Annika S. Hansen

From Congo to Kosovo:

Civilian Police in Peace Operations

Adelphi Paper 343

Oxford University Press, Great Clarendon Street, Oxford OX2 6DP
Oxford   New York
Athens Auckland Bangkok Bombay Calcutta Cape Town
Dar es Salaam Delhi Florence Hong Kong Istanbul Karachi
Kuala Lumpur Madras Madrid Melbourne Mexico City
Nairobi Paris Singapore Taipei Tokyo Toronto
and associated companies in
Berlin Ibadan

Oxford is a trade mark of Oxford University Press

Published in the United States
by Oxford University Press Inc., New York

First published May 2002 by **Oxford University Press** for
The International Institute for Strategic Studies
Arundel House, 13–15 Arundel Street, Temple Place, London WC2R 3DX
www.iiss.org

Director John Chipman
Editor Mats R. Berdal
Copy Editor Charles Hebbert

British Library Cataloguing in Publication Data
Data available

Library of Congress Cataloguing in Publication Data

ISBN 0-19-851673-8
ISSN 0567-932x

Contents

Glossary

ASF	Auxiliary Security Force (Somalia)
CIU	Criminal Investigation Unit (Kosovo)
CPD	Civilian Police Division (UN)
CPU	Civilian Police Unit (UN)
ECOWAS	Economic Community of West African States
FAd'H	Haitian Armed Forces/Forces Armées d'Haiti
FMLN	Farabundo Marti National Liberation Front (El Salvador)
HNP	Haitian National Police/Police Nationale d'Haiti
ICITAP	International Criminal Investigative Training Assistance Program
INTERFET	International Force in East Timor
IFOR	Implementation Force (Bosnia-Herzegovina)
IPM	International Police Monitors (Haiti)
IPSF	Interim Public Security Forces (Haiti)
IPTF	International Police Task Force (Bosnia-Herzegovina)
KFOR	Kosovo Force
KPC	Kosovo Protection Corps
KPS	Kosovo Police Service
MIST	Military Information Support Teams (Haiti)
MNF	Multinational Military Force (Haiti)
MONUA	United Nations Observer Mission in Angola
OHCHR	Office of the High Commissioner for Human Rights (UN)
ONUC	United Nations Operation in Congo

ONUMOZ	United Nations Operation in Mozambique
ONUSAL	United Nations Observer Mission in El Salvador
OSCE	Organisation for Security and Cooperation in Europe
PNC	Policia Nacional Civil (El Salvador and Guatemala)
ROEs	Rules of Engagement
RUC	Royal Ulster Constabulary (Northern Ireland)
SFOR	Stabilisation Force (Bosnia-Herzegovina)
SOC	State of Cambodia
SOPs	Standard Operating Procedures
SPUs	Special Police Units
SRSG	Special Representative of the Secretary-General
TA	Transitional Administrator (Eastern Slavonia)
TPF	Transitional Police Force (Eastern Slavonia)
UNAMET	United Nations Mission in East Timor
UNAMIR	United Nations Assistance Mission for Rwanda
UNAVEM	United Nations Angola Verification Mission
UNCJS	UN Criminal Justice Standards for Peacekeeping Police
UNFICYP	United Nations Peacekeeping Force in Cyprus
UNHCR	United Nations High Commission for Refugees
UNIP	United Nations International Police, also referred to as UNMIK Police (Kosovo)
UNITA	National Union for the Total Independence of Angola
UNITAF	Unified Task Force (Somalia)
UNMIBH	United Nations Mission in Bosnia and Herzegovina
UNMIH	United Nations Mission in Haiti
UNMIK	United Nations Mission in Kosovo
UNOSOM	United Nations Operation in Somalia
UNPREDEP	United Nations Preventive Deployment Force (Macedonia)
UNPROFOR	United Nations Protection Force (Croatia/Bosnia)
UNPSG	United Nations Police Support Group (Eastern Slavonia)
UNSMIH	United Nations Support Mission in Haiti
UNTAC	United Nations Transitional Authority in Cambodia
UNTAES	United Nations Transitional Administration in Eastern Slavonia, Baranja and Western Sirmium
UNTAET	United Nations Transitional Administration in East Timor

UNTAG	United Nations Transitional Authority Group (Namibia)
UNTEA	United Nations Temporary Executive Authority (West New Guinea/Irian Jaya)
WEU	Western European Union

Introduction

Civilian police officers were first deployed as part of a UN peace operation in the Congo in the early 1960s. They were a haphazard supplement to the military observers who were entrusted with the actual peacekeeping mission. From the 1960s to the late 1980s, civilian police were deployed only sporadically and their task was to accompany local police on patrols, monitor police behaviour and in some cases give advice. The revival of international civilian police operations began in Namibia in 1989, where monitoring the restructuring and performance of local police was a minor element in the United Nations Transitional Authority Group (UNTAG). It moved on to training and reform missions in El Salvador, Haiti, Cambodia, Somalia, Eastern Slavonia and Bosnia-Herzegovina and elsewhere: civilian police components were gradually assigned a specific role within a peace operation and were deployed strategically in the pursuit of the overall goals of the mission as a whole. This trend culminated in the UN Civil Administrations in Kosovo and East Timor, where international civilian police temporarily replaced local security forces and assumed responsibility for maintaining law and order. This role is known as executive policing because the international police officers in these circumstances are solely responsible for executing and enforcing the law. It represents a major step in that executive policing places high demands on civilian police operations and disempowers the host state by taking over its monopoly on legitimate violence. As a result, the *executive policing role* has a tendency to overshadow the more traditional efforts at monitoring and training, i.e. the *non-executive* role of civilian police.

Police assistance is nothing new. Bilateral police assistance was common in the 1960s and resembled the training and reform activities that UN police contingents have engaged in since the 1990s and which are currently in the spotlight. Historically, assistance to police forces was provided by external powers in order to prop up unstable client regimes or strengthen insurgency groups. When, however, these police forces and, implicitly, the assistance for them were linked to human rights abuses, police support became taboo for many donors. It was also subject to restrictions due to more general concerns about the 'sacrosanct' principle of non-intervention in the internal affairs of other states. Clearly, this attitude has changed and more intrusive outside intervention has become politically acceptable: internal security forces are seen as institutions of public service and protection that form the backbone of a democratic society. Although presented as a noble cause, the change in perception is closely linked to the view that a reform of internal security structures is perhaps the best safeguard against continued instability and the threat of refugee flows and organised crime that emanates from conflict areas.

From being an afterthought in UN peace operations, international civilian police and the wider task of maintaining law and order have become one of the major pillars of building peace in war-torn societies. Missions that were considered daring and unacceptably intrusive only a few years ago now proceed as a matter of course. The operation in Kosovo and the less publicised one in East Timor triggered none of the consternation that they would have aroused only half a decade ago.

This paper will review the record of achievements of – predominantly UN-led – civilian police operations from the first deployment to the Congo in the 1960s. In the course of the review, it restates criticism where justified, identifies key challenges to future operations and suggests what can be expected if these are not met. Realistic expectations are essential since civilian police operations are here to stay. The ensuing question is how international organisations and their contributing members can make the best of difficult conditions and which types of tasks and operations are more propitious than others. The paper refers to a range of cases, mainly covering the period 1989–2001, from the most cited and best documented peace operations in Haiti, Cambodia, El Salvador, Bosnia-Herzegovina and Kosovo, to the less well-known ones in Eastern Slavonia, Somalia, East Timor and Mozambique.

Criticism of UN Civilian Police is all the rage at present and is voiced by a wide range of observers in international news media, NGOs and research institutions. Most of the criticism takes the shape of calls for more policemen, preferably with heavier equipment and more extensive authority. And this certainly appears to be the favoured 'easy' remedy for undeniable shortfalls in the efforts of international organisations, first and foremost the UN, to establish and maintain law and order in war-torn societies, as was seen in Kosovo. Rather than devising a sound concept of what was to be achieved by the international police and how, the challenges that resulted from the sweeping mandate of the United Nations Mission in Kosovo (UNMIK) were addressed by deploying a police force of unprecedented size.

However, much of the criticism fails to recognise the novelty of the role that international police were asked to play in Kosovo and East Timor, replacing the local police and taking on responsibility for law and order, which in practice included assuming primary responsibility for judicial and penal functions. As Chapter One will show, before these two missions, international civilian police had only assumed responsibility for these functions for very brief spells and in limited geographic areas. Critics have not understood the fundamental shift that is involved in enforcing the law as opposed to merely monitoring how local police enforce it.

Understanding the distinction between executive and non-executive roles is critical for assessing the extent to which international civilian police have been successful. For the undeniable value of civilian police tends to get lost amidst undiscerning commentary. In the public eye, law and order is limited to ensuring respect for human rights and providing effective protection for the population of 'exposed' areas rather than the intricate range of activities that international civilian police carry out when they alone are responsible for enforcing the law. An undifferentiated view of the tasks and objectives of police deployment prevents an accurate and thorough understanding of the challenges, pitfalls and the potential of civilian police in peace operations. The nature of the challenges encountered – and the resources and skills needed to meet them – all vary in accordance with whether or not the civilian police component has full operational authority for maintaining law and order.

There are clearly significant shortfalls in the deployment of international civilian police in peace operations. Shortfalls are both quantitative – it is difficult to recruit and maintain a sufficient number of policemen – and qualitative – those deployed often do not have the skills for the level of violence that characterises war-torn societies. The shortfalls are often crippling to a mission and are difficult to remedy. Given this bleak outlook, the question is whether the benefits of deploying civilian police outweigh the difficulties and justify the costs. The paper argues that civilian police have an important role to play, but that their working environment can be significantly improved. An important change concerns the cooperation between civilian police, the military forces, formed police units, such as the Gendarmerie or the Carabinieri, and indigenous security forces. There is a real potential for alleviating some of the shortcomings of international civilian police by refining the division of labour among different security forces and strengthening joint planning arrangements. Developments in civilian policing so far have brought essential improvements in the practical organisation of civilian police operations as implemented in Kosovo and East Timor. Nonetheless, the scope of police missions is developing at breakneck pace and efforts to formulate guidelines for civilian police deployment are struggling to keep up.

Complex though the logistical details of these operations might be, the harder problems to tackle are generally of a political nature. Therefore, this paper addresses the issue of the politics behind mandates and offers a separate discussion of the local context, which is a pivotal factor for international policing. Whether there is a police force in-theatre that is to be reformed or whether international organisations have taken on the responsibility for law and order themselves, internal security is a highly political matter. At a local level, civilian police operations interfere in the local balance of power, and the police officers' ability to carry out their tasks is affected by the levels of insecurity and crime they encounter. The effectiveness of these operations can also be impaired at the international level, when contributing governments lack the political will and commitment to engage in planning and implementation of police missions and to provide the necessary resources for the job. Another major political factor is the willingness and the ability of governments and other donors to develop a cohesive approach that provides continuity and clout to the civilian police. As will be suggested at various points throughout the paper, it is highly important, but also very difficult, to maintain an enabling political environment for civilian police operations.

The evolution of international intervention in internal security matters has been remarkable. Since the early 1990s, civilian police missions all over the world have become more intrusive, more comprehensive and play a greater role within peace operations. At the same time, expectations have risen out of step with international organisations' – such as the UN or the OSCE's – ability to conduct police operations effectively. On the surface, promoting the rule of law and enhancing the police capacity of the authorities in a conflict area may be a matter of selecting and training staff. In practice, however, it is a process of fundamentally changing the dynamic of a society.

For a long time, the planners of police missions and practitioners alike have focused excessively on technical and structural aspects of police reform – on the size, organisation and equipment of a local police force. Only gradually have they realised that consolidating the rule of law involves building the population's confidence in the police and in its own ability to play an active role in assuring its personal security. The rule of law also involves bringing about a shift in the self-perception of a local police force from an instrument of the state to a public service institution. This shift is only viable when it is supported by a corresponding shift to a propitious political context in which the police enforce the law independent of political agendas. In short, creating a democratic civilian police force is part of a major exercise in building and transforming states. Policy makers and critics have to recognise that civilian police missions are an integral part of a vast and ambitious project of conflict management and political and socio-economic development. Ideally, this recognition will bring with it a more realistic understanding of what police missions can hope to achieve in a war-torn society, so that policy makers, observers and researchers alike can assess the impact of international efforts in accordance with standards that are tempered by expectations generated on the ground.

The eventual success or failure of the missions in Kosovo and East Timor is likely to have a significant impact on the extent to which international organisations will be willing to take on executive policing functions. In the most extreme case – where the UN has exclusive operational authority – enthusiasm might well dwindle when it becomes clear just how ill-equipped the UN is for assuming this degree of involvement. However, maintaining law and order is a key element of peace building and will remain a challenge in the years to come. The question is not whether, but how it should be undertaken and where the limitations of international engagement lie.

Chapter 1

The Evolution of Civilian Policing

Leaving aside the early deployment of civilian police in the Congo and Cyprus, the role of UN civilian police has expanded dramatically in the course of the 1990s. It moved from monitoring in Namibia in 1989–90, to reform and training in, for instance, El Salvador and finally to maintaining law and order – executive policing – in Kosovo in the late 1990s. As indicated in the introduction, the expansion of the international police's role has been tremendous – from merely observing police forces to investigating crimes and arresting criminals in a conflict area – and has not been matched by a corresponding 'doctrinal' or conceptual development to guide these operations. Nor has it been accompanied by an evolution in planning and operational capacity, either at UN headquarters or in the capitals of contributing governments. As a result, the UN is carrying out far more ambitious operations but has only been able to make marginal improvements in the conduct and understanding of such operations. Although lessons are sometimes identified, they are seldom implemented in new civilian police missions and planning remains largely non-existent. Moreover, as we shall see throughout the paper, decisions on the precise nature of a mission ultimately depend on the national political interests of Security Council members and other contributing governments.

International organisations become involved in policing because indigenous public security structures are dysfunctional or malfunctioning, biased or corrupt in the wake of a conflict.[1] Such conflict often continues to permeate the law and order framework

– in the form of residual ethnic tension, vested interests that emerged from the war economy, distorted military-police relations and the legacy of police behaviour prior to and during the conflict. For example, the history of brutality and arbitrary behaviour of the public security forces in El Salvador meant both that the population did not consider the police impartial and that the government did not stop trying to exercise control over the domestic security forces. The legacy of relations between the citizens, the government and the security forces, had clear implications for the reform plans negotiated between the donors of police assistance and the authorities in El Salvador.[2]

The original scope of an international policing operation is determined by the state of the indigenous law and order arrangements – i.e. the existence and state of the police force(s), courts and prisons, a legal code and civilian supervision mechanisms. Although a formal system of law and order might not exist, informal networks invariably do. Indeed, it is a fallacy to believe that there will be a complete – and certainly not a lasting – security vacuum. There may not be an official police force or a formal and generally accepted legal code but there will be other corrective social mechanisms to maintain some degree of order. If the state is unable to fill the vacuum, alternative non-state security providers, such as vigilante groups, or informal rules for social interaction, will emerge. Examples are the traditional clan structures and the shadow society established in the 1990s in Kosovo or the rule of law enforced by the Farabundo Marti National Liberation Front (FMLN) in the areas under its control in El Salvador and by the National Union for the Total Independence of Angola (UNITA) in its territory in Angola. Rather than stepping in to fill a vacuum, international police and civilian staff are often tasked with providing a system of formal law and order which competes with informal indigenous networks that are either traditional or have sprung up as a result of conflict.

The Initial Missions: Civilian Police as Monitors and Advisors

The role of the first civilian police operations was limited to observing and reporting, and they were numbered and equipped accordingly. Typical activities included accompanying patrols, sometimes in small groups, mostly as individual monitors. Civilian police monitors – as they were aptly called – would not intervene themselves but would give advice and report on human rights violations to either the UN Special Representative, the Mission Head or the Force Commander. The term 'CivPol', which dominates the UN terminology on international policing, was coined in 1964 in the context of the UN peacekeeping mission in Cyprus. It marked the first time a UN Civilian Police was designed as part of the mission.[3] As of January 2001, 33 civpol officers were still serving with the United Nations Peacekeeping Force in Cyprus (UNFICYP).

A new era of civilian police operations began with the UN mission in Namibia in 1989–1990, which set the tone for the initial civilian police monitoring missions. The civilian police monitors in the United Nations Transitional Authority Group (UNTAG) in Namibia were asked to monitor the South West African Police (SWAPOL), which was responsible for 'maintaining law and order in an efficient, professional and non-partisan way'.[4] The 1,500 strong UNTAG contingent also provided support during the elections and assisted the military components in monitoring the ceasefire. This blurring of military and police tasks characterises early civpol operations and recurred especially clearly in the UN operation in Cambodia.

Three main tasks for civilian police monitors emerged from UNTAG in the early 1990s: accompanying local police in performing their duties; receiving and investigating public complaints about the police; and supervising investigations conducted by local police. The United Nations Operation in Mozambique (ONUMOZ) was the next substantial mission in Africa and was based on the model established by the Namibia mission. It was also a precursor to later training and police reform missions, in that civpol were to 'monitor and verify the process of reorganisation and retraining of the Quick Reaction Police'.[5] It is important to note, however, that ONUMOZ was not itself conducting the training.

To outside observers the trend towards the UN civilian police's more expanded role and greater responsibility might suggest that more limited missions no longer take place. This is not accurate: the United Nations Mission in East Timor (UNAMET) is a recent, but very typical example of an 'old-style' mission, in that it was limited to monitoring the behaviour of the Indonesian police in the run-up to the referendum in East Timor. Nevertheless, the civilian police's monitoring role has indeed evolved since Namibia in 1989, moving from haphazard observation to more focused 'measuring' of performance against a set of criteria. The criteria used to assess local police performance have become more consistent and explicit over the years. Monitoring now reviews local police in terms of their compliance with internationally accepted standards of human rights and UN Criminal Justice Standards (UNCJS).[6]

The ability to monitor local police forces – which had become an integral part of civilian police operations by the early 1990s – was severely tested in Cambodia. Early plans for the United Nations Transitional Authority in Cambodia (UNTAC) emphasised the lessons learnt in Namibia: that through their day-to-day patrolling the civilian police monitors had been more effective than the military peacekeepers or SWAPOL, the local security force, in instilling trust in the population. However, UNTAC's mandate included a subtle but telling difference. Rather than just issuing a monitoring mandate, the civilian police in UNTAC were to 'supervise and control' indigenous police forces.[7] Yet there was no provision in UNTAC's mandate for reforming local police forces.

Aside from the fact that the world was simply not ready for more extensive intervention in the internal matters of another state in the early 1990s, there was a good argument in favour of unarmed monitors and limited mandates. Where civilian police monitors did make progress, it was often due to their lack of power, since they did not represent a threat to the local police and/ or the host governments of Namibia, Cambodia and Mozambique – who themselves were struggling to consolidate power in the wake of a civil war. As John McFarlane, a researcher on Australian police involvement, points out, 'the influence and effectiveness of CivPol is based on moral authority rather than the threat of force'.[8] Naturally, the dynamic of well-meaning advice and graceful acceptance worked only as long as there was sufficient cooperation on the part of the local police. In Namibia and in Cambodia, UN CivPol was hampered by lack of cooperation from the SWAPOL and the State of Cambodia (SOC) police respectively. In fact, the unwillingness of the SOC police to maintain law and order in an impartial manner was a principal factor for civpol's first step down the slippery slope of executive policing in Cambodia. In Namibia, SWAPOL's resistance to external supervision also illustrated that the civilian police were dependent on reinforcement from their military counterparts in the mission and even more so on continued political pressure on the South African government, the political masters of SWAPOL.

The resistance that civpol met when attempting to monitor police forces in Cambodia also raised the question of whether civilian police should be armed. One of the main arguments against carrying arms was the desire to underline the civilian character of policing and the belief that bearing arms would contribute to escalating violence in an already volatile context. A further worry was that contributing governments would be reluctant to provide personnel for what would then be considered dangerous missions. This issue remained unresolved until the executive missions in Kosovo and East Timor where it was considered inevitable that the civilian police carry arms.

One of the most serious challenges that emerged from these initial missions was the issue of unqualified personnel. Essentially, monitoring and advising meant that local police forces could witness the international civilian police's professionalism and follow their example. This was the most successful aspect of monitoring missions, but its effectiveness depended greatly on the quality of the staff deployed. For the international civilian police rely on close relations with the indigenous police force and the development of a 'professional camaraderie'[9] in their monitoring activity. As the civilian police gained a higher profile and took on a bigger share of the mission, their quality was ever more closely scrutinised. When problems with low quality staff and incidents such as the misconduct of a few civilian police personnel surfaced in Cambodia, the UN defined minimum standards for the selection of international staff.[10] As will be discussed in more detail below, other factors, such as the lack of planning, inconsistent support from contributing capitals and the pressure for rapid deployment, have entailed that the minimum standards have in themselves done little to alleviate the problem of policemen unsuitable for international deployment.

Involvement in Police Reform

Efforts to reform the structure of a police organisation were novel to the civilian police's role in peace operations. Operations such as those in Namibia and Mozambique led to police reform as a natural continuation of monitoring. On these missions the reform efforts, which continued after the withdrawal of the UN mission, were bilateral: for instance, police training in Mozambique was conducted by the Spanish Guardia Civil, rather than by members of the UN peacekeeping mission. Nevertheless, the monitoring of police behaviour in the initial missions in Namibia, Mozambique and Cambodia was the first step towards UN involvement in police reform. From simply observing the extent to which human rights were respected, the advice offered by the UN took on more of a binding stance, and a pattern emerged of forcing compliance from recipient authorities through incentives or threats of punishment. The shift from monitoring to advising local authorities on reform also meant that international civilian police no longer simply assessed the performance of an individual policeman, but reviewed the organisation and structure of the indigenous police as a whole. The international presence touched on the way the governments of El Salvador, Bosnia, Haiti or Mozambique exercised their power and to what extent they sanctioned human rights violations by the police forces under government control. In that way, the UN advice was highly sensitive and could be perceived as more threatening to a government whose basis and instruments of power were under scrutiny.

The nature of civilian police deployments began to change with the United Nations Observer Mission in El Salvador (ONUSAL) when reform was made a pivotal element for the first time. William Stanley states that ONUSAL represented 'the most radical attempt to date to put internal security forces under civilian control' and that the 'international community provided unprecedented levels of technical assistance, training, on-the-job supervision, and material assistance to the new police force'.[11] In fact, ONUSAL was a curious mix between a 'traditional' monitoring mandate and the commission to create a brand new police force. The civilian police component was to monitor the compliance of the old National Police (PN) with human rights standards, until they had selected, trained and begun monitoring newly deployed Policia Nacional Civil (PNC) officers. It is important to note that during the two-year transition period operational authority remained firmly in the hands of the old police force, despite the fact that the force was not acceptable to the parties and did not meet democratic standards. In other words, ONUSAL had no mandate for executive policing but instead bought time to build a new force by temporarily leaving the old one in place. ONUSAL was considered a success in terms of setting up the new national police force, although its achievements were overshadowed by high crime rates and the continued meddling of the El Salvadorian military. The improvements were nonetheless sufficient to convince contributing governments that civilian police deployment in a peacekeeping operation had come to stay.

While ONUSAL attracted most of the attention, several other operations were initiated at about the same time – 1992–94. There was UNAVEM II, followed by UNAVEM III in Angola; ONUMOZ in Mozambique; UNTAC in Cambodia; UNAMIR in Rwanda, which conducted a police training programme in 1994–6; UNOSOM II in Somalia; the first of what became a series of missions in Haiti; and the United Nations Protection Force (UNPROFOR), the first of several missions with civilian police involvement in the Balkans. Of these missions, the ones in Rwanda, Somalia and Haiti had explicit mandates for training indigenous police forces while the other operations still focused on monitoring. In May 1993, the growing role of civilian police also manifested itself in the creation of a separate Civilian Police Unit at the UN Department of Peacekeeping Operations (DPKO). The unit was 'to plan and co-ordinate all matters relating to civpol activities in UN peacekeeping operations'.

A recognition of the integral role of civilian police in peace operations also resulted in organisational changes being proposed at the UN headquarters in early 2001, which reflected the comprehensive operations in Kosovo and East Timor and the recommendations in the 'Brahimi Report'.[12] This report suggested that the

Civilian Police Unit be upgraded to a Civilian Police Division (CPD) and its head promoted to the same level as the military advisor to the Under-Secretary General for Peacekeeping in DPKO, but implementation has been delayed due to a reluctance in the General Assembly to allocate more funds to peacekeeping measures. (The change in name – to Division – has been made but this is hardly the upgrade the report recommended since its head has not been promoted.) Despite the moves towards involvement in police reform, the unit's brief in 1995 was still to 'monitor local police to ensure they carry out their tasks without discrimination against any nationality and with full respect for the human rights of all residents in the mission area'.[13]

The need to reformulate the role of civilian police operations took a long time to be recognised. Gradually, however, the extensive involvement in numerous missions contributed to the development of the 'SMART' concept – Support for human rights, Monitoring and Reporting, and Advising and Training – introduced in 1995 as a basic guideline for international civilian police operations. In practice, the SMART concept means, for example, that police officers involved in police reform in the context of a UN peacekeeping operation define – or assist local authorities in defining – the size and structure of the future police force. Since the early 1990s, most operations that have taken on police reform have also involved setting up – or supporting local authorities in setting up – police academies, developing curricula, and so forth. In this context, the International Criminal Investigative Assistance Program (ICITAP), a US government agency created in 1986 and designed to develop investigative skills and police management and training in conflict-prone and conflict-ridden countries, has played an important role. ICITAP has promoted the standardisation of teaching tools to be used in police academies in mission areas and has thereby enabled organisations other than ICITAP to set up academies more quickly, as was the case for the OSCE police training programme in Kosovo. In virtually all cases – El Salvador, Haiti, Bosnia-Herzegovina, Kosovo and elsewhere – the international civilian police was involved in vetting, recruiting and selecting police officers for the new force, as well as teaching at the police academies, which was complemented by field training.

Subsequently, the performance of the newly deployed police was monitored and specialised follow-up training conducted, such as in Haiti, where courses in crowd control were held.[14]

From the Namibia operation onwards, virtually all cases underline the importance of military-police relations in war-torn societies. As Rachel Neild points out, 'police reforms have tended to be undertaken in the first place because of the need to replace military or other combatant forces, and only in later phases as part of a broader effort to establish a functional criminal justice system and the rule of law'.[15] Often the prior conflict – or established approaches to providing internal security – result in a blurred distinction between the military and the police. Especially when engaging in reforming and restructuring or in establishing indigenous police forces, the international civilian police has to deal with various military influences on the police forces, including military personnel, military culture and doctrine and military equipment.

This problem of distinguishing between military and police operations has surfaced in a number of recent missions. In Angola, for example, although both the armed forces and the various police forces formally existed as distinct entities, they were not clearly identifiable. All were equally militarised and participated more or less directly in the civil war. Therefore, when monitoring the behaviour of the Angolan National Police, the civilian police component of UNAVEM III was effectively trying to monitor part of a military campaign. In Haiti – as in El Salvador – there was no clear separation between military and police. Security forces had always been more or less generic and functioned mainly as an instrument of oppression rather than as one of public service. Haiti is a typical example of a former colony in which haphazard security structures that were left behind – in this case after the US intervention (1914–35) – became the prime tool for consolidating the power of the post-intervention government.[16] In Bosnia-Herzegovina, the police force had increased in size to about 54,000 during the war. Moreover, it was militarised in terms of its level of armament, its doctrine and outlook; because of its involvement in the war, it was also ethnically divided. However, in contrast to Haiti and El Salvador, the pre-war police in the Federal Republic of Yugoslavia had been separate from the military and was well-educated, well-trained and effective, with a distinct professional identity.[17] Arguably, the UN therefore had an easier starting-point in Bosnia-Herzegovina than in Haiti or El Salvador, as it could build on the rudiments of a civilian police force in its police reform efforts after the war.

As a result of the close link between military and police forces, most peace processes call for the demobilisation of excess military personnel. During demobilisation, there is a danger that the newly established or reformed police forces become the net into which demobilised soldiers fall. Initially, this is an attractive option for international peacekeepers and civilian staff overseeing demobilisation and reintegration: an obvious and potentially rapid transition and a way in which to keep former combatants out of criminal circles.

However, there are several pitfalls. First, demilitarising police forces requires refocusing them on public rather than national security. This involves stripping them of military doctrines, organ-isational structures and equipment, all of which could be difficult to accomplish and be undermined by the presence of soldiers in the police force, as they often find it difficult to leave behind ways of thinking established during their military service. In Kosovo, one alternative was to collect former KLA members in a new body called the Kosovo Protection Corps (KPC), which was designed to be distinct from military and police structures and be responsible for reconstruction and relief operations in future crises stemming from natural disasters, such as floods and so forth.

Second, the problem of reintegration is only superficially solved as post-war authorities are saddled with an excessively large and financially unsupportable police force. Although the setting up of the KPC went smoothly, problems persisted with funding and with defining the KPC's role.[18] In time, the reduction of police forces may become an unavoidable and highly sensitive and destabilising political issue. The protests and accusations trig-gered by the Croatian government's announcement of cuts in police manpower in the summer of 2001 are a case in point.[19]

These pitfalls notwithstanding, the optimism generated by ONUSAL triggered calls for even deeper involvement in 'peace building'.[20] In Cambodia the UN quickly withdrew after the elections in May 1993, not willing to enter the quagmire of long-term democratisation efforts. However, since then, police reform has come to be seen as a component in development and governance issues and a key to peace building and democratisation efforts. The role of the police in relation to the other elements of the security sector, i.e. the courts and prisons, has also been recognised and so-called security sector reform programmes have become a specific objective on the agenda of donor agencies and contributing governments. As we shall see below, the missions in Kosovo and East Timor were the first to incorporate a comprehensive approach, in that clear links were established between judicial, penal and police reform from the outset of the peace operations. In Kosovo, for instance, a new 'Police and Justice Pillar' was created in UNMIK in May 2001 to ensure coordination and a cohesive approach to public security.[21]

As missions grew in scope and more multilateral actors became involved in peacekeeping operations, the UN lost its monopoly on international civilian police deployment. Consequently, the tasks that make up the entirety of the police effort began to be divided between several actors. The UN, the OSCE and the EU/WEU have emerged as the most important international organisations that deploy international police. Bilateral donors have of course always been on the scene and are another main source of police assistance, contributing funds, experts, or equipment. Although bilateral donors usually conduct their own reform or monitoring programmes, in agreement with the recipient government, attempts are made to integrate them within or at least coordinate more with, a comprehensive peace operation.

Taking on Responsibility for Law and Order

The context for the deployment of civilian police changed fundamentally in 1999, when UN civil administrations were established in Kosovo and East Timor and maintaining law and order became an integral and inescapable part of the UN's execution of authority in these territories. Although the extent of involvement in executive policing in Kosovo and East Timor was unprecedented, there were tentative forerunners from the very early days of UN peacekeeping. Some early missions were charged with maintaining law and order, but this was limited to very specific circumstances. The first example is UNEF I in the Gaza Strip in early 1957, when the peacekeeping force was effectively maintaining law and order in the transition period following Israeli troop withdrawal. The second example is the deployment of a small Ghanaian police unit and later a large contingent of 400 Nigerian policemen to assist Congolese police and to conduct riot control as part of the United Nations Operation in Congo (ONUC) in 1964/5.

UNTAG in Namibia and UNTAC in Cambodia had also been transitional authorities in name, but were a far cry from what this came to embody in Kosovo and East Timor. And yet, to the limited extent that lessons are identified and become part of the UN's institutional memory, the experiences from Cambodia left the UN's CivPol Unit decidedly apprehensive about the practicality of an executive policing role. UNTAC's mandate had seemed so innocuous: the civilian police component was asked to supervise and control the SOC police on patrol and promote respect for human rights while doing so; to support the electoral process; and to provide security to returnees as part of the resettlement programme.[22] The implementation of the UN civpol mandate was sidetracked when conditions became more unstable and the SOC were increasingly unwilling to cooperate.

Despite the worsening climate, the UN, in particular the Special Representative of the Secretary-General (SRSG) and the Secretary-General, were unwilling to abandon the mission and instead focused their efforts on the planned elections. The civilian police were forced to allocate a greater share of their resources to guarding polling stations and preventing harassment in connection with the election campaign. At its peak, 65% of the UN CivPol staff were engaged in these activities,[23] which meant that the task of monitoring the SOC police suffered. As a result, the SOC police increasingly neglected their duty to maintain law and order impartially. As the international operation could hardly stand by and tolerate the abuses, an unprecedented directive bestowed powers to 'arrest and detain' on to the military component and an already far too thinly stretched civilian police force. Lee Kim and Metrikas write that 'although hundreds of investigations were conducted by civpol officers, prosecution was hampered by excessive reliance on inadequate local public security structures and the absence of impartial judicial mechanisms'.[24] In short, the civilian police component of UNTAC slithered into an executive policing role without a clear objective and without judicial back-up. It is no wonder that this exercise was a complete failure. However, civilian police deployment has come a long way since then and – despite an equal lack of pre-deployment planning – the operations in Kosovo and East Timor bear little resemblance to UNTAC.

The excursion into executive policing forced upon the international military force and police monitors in Haiti was as little planned as the operation in Cambodia. For it soon became clear that the existing security forces were unable to measure up to democratic standards, i.e. did not respect human rights and were not subject to civilian control, and were unacceptable even on a temporary basis. Also, in an effort to purge security forces of potential government opponents, the Haitian government insisted that all military officers had to pass the entrance exam of the newly established Police Academy in Port-au-Prince before joining the newly created national police force. Although they were not officially banned, only 30–40 former Haitian Armed Forces (FAd'H) managed to pass the Academy exam, so that the military had a very limited presence in the Haitian National Police (HNP).[25] This created a vacuum, which meant that until the first police officers had completed the police academy training courses, the international civilian police and the US-led Multinational Military Force (MNF) were responsible for maintaining law and order in the initial phase of the operation alongside the Interim Public Security Forces (IPSF). The situation in Somalia was similar in that an Auxiliary Security Force (ASF) based on established Somali police structures had operational authority, but the remaining gaps in law enforcement were filled by UNITAF, in particular its Military Police component.

The more immediate predecessor for the missions in Kosovo and East Timor was the United Nations Transitional Administration in Eastern Slavonia, Baranja and Western Sirmium (UNTAES) in Eastern Slavonia. The success of UNTAES, where the UN had established a trusteeship in the shadow of the higher profile mission in neighbouring Bosnia-Herzegovina, was encouraging. Police reform had run smoothly – aside from continued, albeit decreasing – attacks on the Serb minority – and the international operation had managed to complete its work on schedule. Members of the Security Council believed that if only the UN in conjunction with other international organisations could take control of all the threads of 'peace building', all would be well.

Therefore, the 'Security Council ... in both Kosovo and East Timor, vested in the UN complete legislative and executive authority over the territories and peoples concerned. In other words, the UN has been asked, as in a 'trusteeship', to be the government and is performing all the tasks one might expect of a government'.[26] As indicated above, providing public security was an essential part of acting as the government. As a result, the UN – together with other international organisations, such as the OSCE and the EU – was called upon to carry out investigations, make arrests, direct traffic, patrol borders, gather, analyse and use criminal intelligence as well as forensic evidence, train local police and manage the organisation and administration of the police force.

The UN missions in East Timor and Kosovo had to contend with three main challenges. First, there was the difficulty in recruiting and deploying a sufficient number of staff in a short period of time. When it became clear that civilian police would not be in place early on, KFOR stepped in, making arrests and detaining a large number of prisoners, just as INTERFET (the International Force in East Timor) had done in East Timor.[27] Second, the range of jobs that would have to be fulfilled as part of the civilian police's responsibility for maintaining law and order, i.e. an executive policing role, was disregarded in both Kosovo and East Timor. In the first weeks and months of UNMIK and UNTAET, it emerged that enforcing the law was far more complex than fulfilling a monitoring role or even reforming local police forces. Both missions continuously struggled to match specialised skills with available positions and urgent needs within the civilian police contingent. And third, it became very clear just how interdependent effective law enforcement and police reform and progress in rebuilding the judicial sector were.

Researchers and practitioners at the UN argue that executive policing is inevitable when there is no local police force to monitor or train. As a result, conditions on the ground – in addition to the political considerations of contributing governments – determine whether the mandate is limited to reform and restructuring, i.e. non-executive policing, or includes executive policing. For example, practitioners and researchers point to the perceived vacuum in Kosovo, where the predominantly Serb police forces had been withdrawn and the existing criminal law was seen as tainted and ostensibly unacceptable to the Kosovo Albanian population. Similarly, courts and prisons, which had been dominated by Serb staff, were in dire need of reform. While the argument that there was a gap that could only be filled by external security forces, such as peacekeepers or civilian police, makes sense – as it certainly does in East Timor – it is not absolute. The case of El Salvador illustrates that decision-makers at the UN have a choice as to whether they want to take on full responsibility for maintaining law and order. How they make that choice is dependent partly on the historical context (other world events may dictate the level of interest in smaller conflict zones at a given time), and partly on the extent to which Security Council members perceive that their interests are at stake in a given conflict area, such as in El Salvador.

More importantly, however, the decision is coloured by the level of involvement that decision-makers are comfortable with at the time a decision is taken. In other words, ONUSAL was considered a daring mission of unprecedented scope. At that stage, executive policing simply appeared too intrusive to be considered seriously. Instead, the old National Police retained operational authority for a transitional period of two years until the new indigenous force could be deployed. As in Kosovo, where the Serb police were considered unacceptable to Kosovo Albanians, in El Salvador it was considered impolitic to grant the government's security forces, which had played an active part in the repression during the civil war, significant control over the FMLN and its supporters. Yet, despite the absence of a 'proper' national police force, ONUSAL was limited to monitoring and – unprecedented – training and chose not to take on executive policing tasks.

Similarly, international civilian police temporarily worked alongside existing local police forces in Eastern Slavonia, later replacing them with a newly trained and structured multi-ethnic police force in the area.[28] A critical difference in the case of Kosovo was that the international community had essentially taken sides in the conflict – in the bombing campaign of spring 1999 – and had branded the retreating Serb security forces as war criminals. In that way, the option of relying on some Serb public security presence for a transitional period was ruled out not only as unacceptable to the Kosovo Albanians, but equally as politically unacceptable to NATO and the United States. In effect, the international community brought upon itself the need to take a much more active part in policing the country through its own involvement in the conflict.

When distinguishing between non-executive roles, namely monitoring, training, restructuring and reform and executive policing, it is important to remember that the efforts of the international civilian police are cumulative rather than consecutive. In other words, the fact that the UNMIK police took on operational authority in the maintenance of law and order did *not* mean that monitoring and training activities ceased. Monitoring, training, reform and restructuring form the essential foundation for any executive policing operation, in that these activities are the ones that build local law enforcement capacity and ultimately allow the international mission to go home.

Nonetheless, the distinction between executive and non-executive roles can sometimes become blurred. There are examples of monitoring and training activities venturing dangerously close to executive policing. For instance, the International Police Task Force (IPTF) in Bosnia-Herzegovina began investigating human rights abuses by the Bosnian police and assisted local authorities in their investigations.[29] The same was true in El Salvador. Another example is Eastern Slavonia, in which the UN was responsible for civil administration, including among other things, paying the salary of local police forces. Although the civpol component's role was limited to monitoring and training, the support for the stability provided by the military peacekeepers on behalf of the UN could be characterised as operations to maintain law and order. These hazy distinctions notwithstanding, there is a clear conceptual dividing line between monitoring and executive policing. While the international police in the above cases may have strayed towards taking on operational authority, none were full-scale executive policing operations – whether theoretically, legally or operationally.

Finally, it is important to keep in mind that executive policing is ultimately what international police officers do in their domestic setting. It is the other tasks, such as monitoring and advising, that they need to be taught prior to deployment. But what needs to be far better understood is what executive policing entails in the unfamiliar setting of a war-torn society, where the civilian police officers face a particular set of circumstances. Most 'post-conflict' societies are characterised by continued ethnic or political tension, a large number of arms, unemployment, displacement, and the prevalence of organised crime. There is much work to be done in evaluating the performance of international civilian police in an executive role and how policing and police guidelines have to be adjusted to the particular circumstances of war-torn societies.

Chapter 2

Mandate, Doctrine and Politics

The Politics of Mandates

A mandate is a many-splendoured thing. First and foremost, a mandate derives from the Security Council resolution that establishes an operation. In common parlance, the terms 'mandate' and 'Security Council Resolution' are often used synonymously. Depending on what other international organisations are involved, the stipulations of the Security Council Resolution will be complemented by formal decisions taken at the North Atlantic Council (NAC), the OSCE Permanent Council or the European Commission. In any case, the mandate for a peace operation will be a product of political wrangling, mainly between the permanent members of the Security Council who all have different interests and opinions as to which measures ought to be authorised for a given conflict. Therefore, a mandate will always be ambiguous enough to accommodate the various irreconcilable views. In the past, national interests of Security Council members and their cultural affinities or historical ties to one of the parties to a conflict have affected the general tenor of a mandate, including any allocation of blame, and the level of force the peacekeepers will be authorised to apply, rather than the details of police tasks. While the use of force in an operation, for instance, is directly relevant to the military component of a peacekeeping mission, such factors also shape the environment for civilian police deployment.

Civilian police issues were typically more of an afterthought – at least until the UN civil administration projects in East Timor and Kosovo. When authorised in the UN Security Council, civilian police components are usually part of the peacekeeping package rather than a separate operation with its own mandate requirements. There has, however, been a shift from the earlier days of civpol, as characterised by the mandates for Mozambique and El Salvador, where police activities were not mentioned at all despite their key role in the peace process. Later missions in Eastern Slavonia or East Timor, to name just two, explicitly refer to the rule of law, indicating the higher profile that public security issues have assumed in the eyes of decision-makers. SC Resolutions that authorise police-only missions, such as SCRes 1141 (1997) which established the United Nations Civilian Police Mission in Haiti (MIPONUH), are an exception to this trend. These operations are part of what one might call 'serial' missions – so-called because they consist of a series of consecutive missions – and are established solely to monitor local police forces. By the time the next segment of a serial mission is initiated, the mandate has become largely irrelevant to the operation on the ground, which has developed its own parameters in the course of the preceding mission.

Eastern Slavonia is a good example of how the process of defining the mandate took place on the ground rather than in UN headquarters. When the UN transitional administration ended, the UN wanted to consolidate its achievements in the law and order field and authorised a 'police support group' (UNPSG) for a one-time nine-month period. The transition from UNTAES to the UNPSG was very smooth because the decision to initiate a follow-on operation was made well in advance of deployment and followed thorough planning. It was also planned by key people in the police contingent of the existing UNTAES mission who co-operated closely with the Croatian government.[1]

Resources and Funding

Some improvements have been made with regard to understanding how a mandate should address challenges in the field of law and order. However, this has been merely a question of developing adequate vocabulary or terminology as there is still a missing link between the mandate wording and the necessary resources, capabilities and joint planning of an operation. Mandates may be full of good intentions and may take the needs of a war-torn society into account, in the sense that the tasks described do aim at filling perceived security gaps. However, little attention is paid to the extent to which the objectives are realistic and achievable given the capabilities authorised, the resources that are likely to be forthcoming and the actual obstacles on the ground. Thus, the mandate for the civilian police component of UNAVEM III in Angola certainly addressed the needs of public security in the post-Lusaka process. The mandate included the following tasks: overseeing the general law and order situation, disarming and partially demobilising the Angolan National Police (ANP) – including the integration of some members of UNITA and the dissolution of paramilitary groups and special police forces – and verifying the neutrality of the ANP. Although all these were critical to building public security in Angola, they were a tall order in the best of circumstances and virtually impossible for a mere 200–250 unarmed monitors, particularly given the high levels of violence that continued to plague Angola in the wake of the 1994 peace agreement. Similarly, successive operations in Somalia progressed to a more sweeping and more intrusive mandate with a smaller and less muscular force. Although civilian police was explicitly included in the mandate, no capacity was actually assigned to the police component under UNOSOM II.[2]

Whether or not a mandate is considered well-designed has therefore less to do with the wording of the mandate than with the resources that are forthcoming for its implementation. The twin cases of the civil administrations in East Timor and Kosovo illustrate this point as well. Despite similar mandates in terms of establishing local police forces, the calls for assistance for the police academies in East Timor have produced a fraction of the resources that were provided for training institutions in Kosovo. In these cases, it is important to recall that the UN has no independent resources, but depends on contributions from its member states. The value of a mandate is therefore conditioned by the level of political interest among contributing governments. Sustained commitment often depends on the extent to which major contributors feel that they have a stake in the outcome of the conflict. In

Bosnia-Herzegovina and Kosovo, there was a clear will to see the peace processes through to a successful outcome, regardless of the cost. Too much prestige hung in the balance for the external parties involved, especially the United States, where this issue had become an important factor in the 1996 Clinton re-election campaign. On the other hand, this was clearly not the case with Angola, where a failure to secure peace would have had no serious consequences for donors and contributors to UNAVEM III, aside from having to witness renewed suffering which could be put down to the parties' recalcitrance.[3]

Funding is perhaps the most tangible expression of political will. The efforts to strengthen indigenous police capacity in Kosovo developed against the backdrop of the operation in Bosnia-Herzegovina. Whereas assistance to police academies had been neglected and funds were difficult to raise in Bosnia-Herzegovina, the Kosovo Police Service School (KPSS) became one of the centre-pieces in efforts to strengthen the rule of law. Of course, a major difference was that public security issues generally enjoyed a higher profile in Kosovo, not the least because the UN suddenly found itself responsible for maintaining law and order as a necessary element in the civilian administration of the province.[4] The operations in Somalia also reflect this pattern. While early funding for the ASF, such as equipment donations, had come from UNOSOM I, UNITAF, other UN agencies and – notably – the warlords themselves, virtually no funds were forthcoming for UNOSOM II, despite elaborate plans and pledges.[5]

Authorisation and Primacy

The role of politics comes out clearly in the distribution of tasks among international organisations. Most often, the choice of authorising organisation has been random – based on the whims of contributing governments at the time of authorisation rather than on merit, experience or suitability – and made by a very small group of states or even individuals, usually dominated by the United States. For example, NATO took over the military role from the UN in implementing the Dayton Agreement in Bosnia-Herzegovina, as the UN's legitimacy had been undermined during UNPROFOR. Although there was a general sense among contributing governments that the UN had 'failed' in Bosnia, it was the insistence of the United States that their participation would be contingent on the implementation mission being NATO-led, that ruled out all possibility of a UN operation. One should keep in mind that the decision-makers are largely the same, whether the operation is authorised under UN, NATO or OSCE auspices. The main difference is in the core composition of the military or police contingent and in the command and control arrangements.

Thus, operations and the choice of their umbrella organisations have always been and will remain a product of the political preferences of capitals, while the manner of distributing police-related tasks merely elicits a resigned shake of the head from academics and practitioners. In Kosovo, the planners in the UN Civilian Police Unit were informed about their responsibility for an executive policing mission towards the end of the bombing campaign, only a few days before SCRes 1244 was passed and the mission began. Until then, it had been assumed that the OSCE – which was later assigned the task of conducting police training – would be asked to take on the responsibility for executive policing.[6] This would have been the preferred choice of the United States, but had to be abandoned in favour of a UN civilian police component to avoid a Russian veto in the UN Security Council.

The politics of the mandate – and of subsequent implementation – will also be affected when there is a state or group of states which has a special interest in the settlement. Their personal and historical ties to the parties might give them the influence and leverage that the UN lacks. Even more so, some operations were contingent upon the engagement of a few key supporters to get off the ground. The US, Canadian and French role in Haiti; the Spanish, French and Italian involvement in El Salvador; and the Portuguese assistance in East Timor, where Portugal is the single largest donor, are all examples of this.[7]

And yet the UN Security Council retains a singular position as authorising agent. Even when mission planning is driven by other organisations, such as NATO, the UN stamp of approval is still worth securing. In practice, the UN is also the organisation that has the least say in which crisis it takes on. Once a crisis has been brought to the attention of the Security Council, its members are under pressure to act in some way. In the worst case, the UN is considered to have failed if it does not manage to agree on a peacekeeping force.[8] This means that Security Council members are careful not to deal with crises and civil wars where they know that they are not willing to intervene, such as Algeria or Sudan. Alternatively, they may feel pressured – by public opinion or by requests from the General Assembly – into taking virtually symbolic action and authorise a peacekeeping operation to which they do not have the intention of contributing either troops or political backing. The Security Council members thereby reinforce the UN's reputation of being an organisation that is selective, ineffective and prejudiced against developing countries and undermine its credibility.

Juggling contributing organisations is closely linked to the discussion of the division of labour between the military and the police. The post-Dayton mission in Bosnia-Herzegovina was a watershed in many ways. For the first time, the international military and the police force were provided by different organisations, where NATO led the military element in IFOR/SFOR and the United Nations was assigned the main responsibility for the International Police Task Force (IPTF), as part of the United Nations Mission in Bosnia and Herzegovina (UNMIBH). (Although it took place earlier, Haiti is not a counter-example, as the UN's role in the first mission was limited to sanctioning the intervention – it did not itself send forces to Haiti. Instead, the US-led Multinational Force (MNF) and the accompanying International Police Monitors (IPMs) were provided by a 'coalition of the willing' that would prepare the ground for a *subsequent* UN mission.) Despite the inclusion of various international organisations and NGOs in the implementation of peace agreements since the Dayton Agreement of 1995, the responsibility for police has by and large remained in the hands of the UN.

The Mandate in its Local Context

Besides the political wrangling in the Security Council or the North Atlantic Council, the mandate is also determined by the balance of power and the long-term ambitions of the parties in the conflict, their consent to international intervention and the stipulations of the peace agreement. Although decision-makers should certainly develop a better understanding of what is realistically achievable, in practice there is not always much room to define tasks. Some tasks are necessitated by the context of the 'post-conflict' society to which the mission is deployed. Thus, taking on partial or complete operational authority was virtually inescapable in the absence of indigenous police forces in Haiti and East Timor. The question for contributing governments and UN staff is how to prepare better for implementing tasks that may not represent an ideal-type situation but will have to be undertaken nonetheless. In short, the challenge is how to make the best of a messy situation.

In most cases, a mandate is supplemented by a peace agreement or other arrangement entered into by the host government and the international organisation – in most cases the UN – or bilateral supporter. A peace agreement includes demands, guarantees and obligations that the parties and international actors have agreed to fulfil regardless of the official mandate. Usually, the SC Resolution refers to the peace agreement, as was the case in the resolutions establishing the peacekeeping operations in El Salvador and Mozambique.

The struggle over the definition of tasks and the scope of an operation is more difficult while negotiating a peace agreement than during UN Security Council debates. The example of Mozambique is a case in point. The Mozambican government was very reluctant to address the reform of the indigenous police forces and prevented a civilian police component from being included in the peace agreement despite the fact that the existing Mozambican police was in dire need of improvement. The RENAMO resistance movement, on the other hand, supported the presence of civilian police monitors. In the end, a separate agreement with a restricted mandate for a civpol deployment had to be designed.[9] When UN civilian police was introduced, it was based on an initiative by the UN Secretary-General but remained contingent upon a request of the Mozambican government, which was not issued until September 1993, nine months after the SC Resolution that had created ONUMOZ.[10]

The Need for Vision and Flexibility

The mandate is a popular target for critics of peacekeeping operations. A common criticism is that mandates are too vague and lack the necessary financial backing. While it is important to realise that mandates are a compromise between the various interests of Security Council members and other contributing governments and so will always be subject to the kinds of limitations indicated above, one can nonetheless identify certain traits that will make a mandate better or worse. A mandate should identify the key challenges that the peacekeeping operation faces in a conflict area, sketch out *what* is to be achieved by the civilian police within a given operation and *how* it is to be achieved. How the mandate is then implemented is an issue of doctrine, personnel, logistics, pace of deployment and similar issues outlined below.

It is critical that the mandate should form part of an over-arching political vision for the outcome of a conflict. A political reference point is necessary for the mandate to be implemented in a sensible manner. This is particularly true when getting involved in police reform, which, as Rachel Neild points out, requires vision since it spans the spectrum from military to development assistance.[11] This framework will never be precise in all details. Indeed, most recent cases in which civilian police have played a significant part have been ambitious state-building projects that vaguely aim at consolidating democratic forms of government and a system of law and order to match. This hazy ambition is a product of the inability of contributors to agree on defining more specific goals and can introduce a significant tension into the implementation of civilian police operations.

At the very least, a mandate should provide a common framework within which political decisions can be made throughout the implementation phase. This could take the shape of agreed underlying principles. One example is a strategy for dealing with spoilers. In Bosnia-Herzegovina, the international community attempted to send a clear message to political extremists on how their involvement in official capacities would not be tolerated. In the local elections of September 1997, they were successful to the extent of holding fast to a fundamental principle and pursuing it with relative consistency: candidates were struck from party lists when the OSCE, which had responsibility for staging elections, deemed them too nationalistic.

Another example of a fundamental principle is the notion of transferring as much authority as possible into local hands. Only by exercising the minimum executive responsibility that is possible without endangering the peace process will international staff avoid letting governments off the hook. Ultimately, the message of respect for human rights will have to come from the local authorities if it is to be self-sustaining. Consistency on fundamental principles requires continued political commitment, cohesion and political will during the execution of a mission. The operation in Somalia was clearly inhibited by the fact that UN decision-makers, UN staff on the ground and other contributors could not agree on whether resolving public security issues was an important aspect of addressing the conflict situation.[12]

A good mandate for a civilian police operation will also tie in with the rest of the mission. In Haiti, all components of the mission were deliberately assigned the same mandate in order to underline the joint effort and the need for close cooperation.[13] The Cambodian case is the star counter-example. Without judicial back-up within the mission and without sufficient political co-operation to allow access to the Cambodian justice system, UNTAC's attempts to maintain law and order were doomed from the outset.

It is important to note, however, that ambiguity in a mandate can sometimes be a good thing. Many operations benefit from some flexibility, so that they can be adjusted to the realities of a dynamic and changing mission without requiring a new SC Resolution. Instead, the mandate is complemented by directives or additional agreements between the parties and the international actors. The Bosnian case is interesting since it was an essentially self-appointed authority – the Peace Implementation Council (PIC) – that decided on current priorities and interpretations of the mandate at their regular meetings. For instance, the IPTF initially focused on monitoring and reforming local police forces, and only took on monitoring court activity later on in the mission, when the conclusions of the PIC meeting in Madrid in December 1998 stressed the need to address reform in other elements of the security sector in addition to the police. Similarly, the IPTF's mandate became more forceful in its application without changing the mandate itself, once the IPTF began to cooperate more closely with SFOR.

Of course, adaptability must be incorporated into a mandate with caution. In some cases, the flexibility of a mandate was stretched to the extent that it changed the nature of the mission. In the worst case a civpol force could be faced with a mission for which it was not structured nor equipped. The developments in Sierra Leone in 2000 were an extreme case that illustrate the difficulties in generating sufficient political support to move from a peacekeeping to a 'peace enforcement' mandate. A better example was the situation in Cambodia in late 1992. Faced with a deteriorating security situation, the question facing the UN CivPol Unit by November was whether to withdraw entirely or to muddle through, i.e. to reinterpret the mandate. Given the political determination to see the Cambodian elections through, the first alternative was never seriously considered. Instead, UNTAC's mandate completely changed the nature and the priorities of civpol's original mission.

Mandates, Guidelines and Doctrine

Frustrated by the lack of a vision for what the Bosnian police should be like at the end of the reform process – aside from a notion that they should be more 'like us' – IPTF Commissioner Peter Fitzgerald collected his thoughts in the 'Commissioner's Guidance for Democratic Policing in the Federation of Bosnia-Herzegovina' in May 1996. Thinking that there were no standards, however, was a misconception on the part of the commissioner. As early as 1994, the UN Civilian Police Unit had extracted those elements out of existing international human rights instruments that related to police work and formulated the UN Criminal Justice Standards for Peacekeeping Police (UNCJS). Thus, contrary to common belief, internationally recognised documents on police behaviour and legal guidelines did exist.[14] However, it took the civilian police operation in Bosnia-Herzegovina – and Commissioner Fitzgerald's guidelines – to significantly raise UN CivPol's profile and provide a catalyst for consolidating a collection of rules. When the UNPSG follow-on mission to UNTAES began in January 1998, the Police Commissioner in Eastern Slavonia introduced the

UNCJS for the local Croatian police and the Universal Standards of Human Rights for the monitoring activity of the international police. As a result, monitoring became more consistent; monitoring activity was more transparent; and the UNPSG monitors could focus more specifically on crimes related to ethnic tensions.[15]

In mid-2001, the CPD published a new document entitled 'Principles and Guidelines for United Nations Civilian Police'. It revised the UN CivPol Handbook of 1995 and aimed at providing guidance for the extended range of tasks that UN CivPol were being assigned in the late 1990s. The CPD groups the tasks that civilian police might face when reconstituting local police forces in the following manner: training; reform and restructuring; mentor and monitoring; establish and building; and assuming executive power. The Guidelines should not be understood as, nor were they meant to be, a step-by-step handbook. Rather, as their name implies, they were created to steer international civilian police officers through anticipated key challenges and provide a staff from widely diverging backgrounds with a common understanding of what was expected of them. The extensive experience in monitoring and training since the 1960s provides a sound basis for developing guidelines that reflect lessons learned from past operations. On the other hand, there have only been two cases – Kosovo and East Timor – in which a civilian police operation was given a mandate with full operational authority. Moreover, as both of these had been running for barely a year when the Guidelines were written, the empirical basis for the Guidelines on executive policing is far weaker. It remains to be seen how well the suggestions contained in the 2001 document reflect the realities of executive policing and to what extent they are actively used by international civilian police.

Despite its commendable purpose, this document only reflects the understanding of a handful of individuals in a small New York office of the different tasks that international civilian police are asked to perform, what these tasks entail, what their limitations are, etc. In effect, they are guidelines divorced from reality. Very few of the actors involved in the deployment of civilian police – contributing governments, other domestic authorities, individual policemen and mission chiefs – are even aware that guidelines and universal standards exist. Those that do have at best a fragmentary knowledge of their content. Despite all the conceptual effort that has gone into developing guidelines, mandates and tasks are still often not clearly understood by those charged with implementing them.

Moreover, there does not appear to be a discussion on the need for guidelines, what their content ought to be, or how they relate to military doctrine. UN CivPol redefines the parameters for its involvement every time it embarks on a new operation. The Guidelines were an attempt to counteract this 'planning' – for lack of a better word – and deployment pattern, by determining a set of principles that would be applicable in all operations, although exactly how far depended on the circumstances of each particular case. The lack of dialogue and exchange on a potential 'doctrine' for police missions is in stark contrast to the military tradition in which there are clear distinctions between doctrine, Rules of Engagement (ROEs) and operational planning. Military doctrine provides parameters that outline the limits to engagement and the manner in which troops may engage. Within the doctrinal parameters that apply to all operations, specific ROEs are set for a particular peacekeeping mission. The discrepancy between the military and the police is highly problematic, as it leads to misunderstandings during the planning and implementation stages of a joint operation. This is an increasingly serious issue as the UN and its partners, such as NATO or ECOWAS, intervene more forcefully by taking on greater responsibility for maintaining security in a conflict area and they need to cooperate ever more closely in the face of high levels of violence and crime. In short, the potential and necessity for close cooperation between the military and the police – which is discussed in more detail in a later section – is clearly undermined by the lack of a common language and the misunderstandings that result.

Aside from the lack of common understanding between the military and the police with regard to 'doctrine', international police operations are accompanied by confusion and exaggerated expectations among contributing governments, the deployed police staff, the media and the population in war-torn societies. Political decision-makers often do not provide an overarching strategy, preferring instead to micro-manage. The international police personnel on the ground add their own interpretation, which may or may not be at odds with – stated or implicit – policy aims. A particularly dangerous situation arises when monitoring and training is not kept distinct from executive policing.[16] The nature of a policeman's work and all his past professional experiences have programmed him to intervene when the law is being broken. This sits badly with a 'hands-off' role and it takes thorough preparation, and perhaps inclination and talent, to fulfil a monitoring role well. Preparation, in turn, is only effective when the bigger picture and the purpose of the mission has been understood. Clearly, commonly accepted and understood guidelines are an essential step towards more effective peace operations.

Human Rights as a Standard for Civilian Police Operations

In the uncertainty over the Guidelines and 'doctrine' and how to implement them, human rights have emerged as a more steadfast standard to which civilian police can refer as a conceptual framework for monitoring, reform and law enforcement. Human rights have graduated from being an 'airy-fairy NGO concern' to becoming the centre of gravity for civilian police operations. Francesca Marotta describes how uniformed personnel – be they military or police – were not considered the appropriate champions of human rights and writes that 'in 1992 the idea of using police to train police on *human rights* was all but obvious'.[17] By the late 1990s, human rights had become an integral part of pre-deployment training for international staff, as well as of training courses at local police academies. Civilian police forces are now established actors in the human rights field and are deemed the single most effective agency when it comes to promoting human rights and assessing government compliance with human rights standards.[18] Human rights play an important role in both non-executive and executive policing. Whereas the former means monitoring general police behaviour and integrating respect for human rights into training and development of new police forces, executive policing involves actively enforcing respect for human rights, such as by conducting investigations into crime and corruption. Clearly, the latter is more sensitive – politically and otherwise – than mere monitoring and reporting.

Originally a somewhat abstract concept – there had been 'little or no debate on [human rights in] CIVPOL work'[19]– by 2000 human rights had to some extent been incorporated within and adjusted to the security sector reform agenda. Thus, human rights meant building institutions, including a legal system, that protect human rights. The agenda also incorporates attempts to create awareness among office-holders and populations about the inalienable nature of human rights, in order to make the public security system more accountable.[20] Further, the defence of human rights can provide a basic minimum for assessing international efforts: as international organisations intervene more forcefully and deeply in the affairs of other states, as they do when deploying civilian police, they struggle to maintain their impartiality. Human rights have become an acceptable common denominator that might provide an answer in the search for the fundamental issue that can unite the international approach and form the basis of cohesion and consistency.[21]

In addition to forming the basis for the 'democratic standards' that are used to assess the performance of indigenous police forces, these rules regulate the behaviour of international civpol officers. Human rights advocates have raised the question of accountability and checks on the conduct of international civilian police. Misconduct is an extremely serious concern for civpol and is treated as such. But neither a police commissioner, nor a Special Representative to the Secretary-General in a mission, nor even the Civilian Police Unit (CPU) in New York have any legal powers to punish misconduct. After the guilty staff member has been repatriated, any legal action is in the hands of the home government, which in the vast majority of cases does nothing.[22]

In order to shore up their own standing, civilian police forces are eager to highlight and cite the legal instruments that provide 'impartial' guidelines on the promotion of human rights, the principles of democratic policing and so on. In addition, the compliance of civilian police forces with human rights is usually included in the agreements that define the civilian police force's role, such as the Dayton Agreement.[23] Thus, the Office of the High Commissioner for Human Rights (OHCHR), the United Nations Development Program and human rights organisations are keeping an eye on the international as well as the newly recruited or reformed local police forces. Also, civilian police components now regularly include an internal affairs office that monitors the behaviour of international police officers and takes disciplinary action when necessary. In the early days of UNMIK in Kosovo there were additional challenges to the compliance of external actors with human rights. The UN had taken on the responsibility for civilian administration, including the judicial and penal sector, but was hard pressed to comply with democratic standards of justice, formal arrest procedures etc., given their lack of staff, confusion over applicable law and the absence of functioning judicial institutions. Here, the OSCE mission included a 'Legal Systems Monitoring Section' which acted as a watchdog on the international staff's compliance with human rights.

Finally, it should be noted that Security Council mandates and CPD guidelines are of course limited to civilian police operations authorised by the United Nations. Increasingly, other international organisations, NGOs and bilateral donors are providing police assistance and are involved in the wider field of reconstituting law and order and reforming the judicial and penal systems in war-torn societies. Most have their own mandates, guidelines, procedures and priorities that need to be reconciled with the UN contribution. In the face of a diverse range of actors and programmes, a well-thought out strategic political vision for a conflict area becomes all the more important. The lack of a coherent approach among different contributors can obviously undermine the public security effort as a whole. This is particularly true in a case such as Kosovo, where non-executive tasks, i.e. training the new Kosovo Police Service (KPS), have been allocated to one group of actors, namely the OSCE and the human rights community, and executive tasks, i.e. enforcing the law and providing a secure environment, to others – the UNMIK police and KFOR, including their military and specialised police units.

Quality and Quantity of Staff
Drowning by Numbers

Leaving aside the politics of peacekeeping, the single most important challenge for civilian police has been the recruitment of an
adequate number of qualified staff. Until this problem can be
alleviated, civilian police will not be able to fulfil their mandate,
however well-designed that mandate may be. For the successes
achieved by 'a few good cops' are overshadowed by the ineptness
and misconduct of others. Issues of quality and quantity of staff
may appear somewhat mundane in the face of the greater philo-
sophical questions of the state-building project that is underway,
but they are still important. These issues have also been well
documented in existing assessments of the role of civilian police in
peace operations, but they remain a critical factor hampering the
effectiveness of international civilian police.

The demand for civilian police in peace operations has risen
dramatically in the space of a few years. Although a large number
of staff were deployed in 1993, when there were seven ongoing
missions – one of which, UNTAC, had 3,500 civilian police – the
proportion of civpol staff within a UN peace operation has grown
markedly. According to figures in the Brahimi Report, civilian
police now make up 24% of staff – military and civilian – in the
field.[24] In the early 1990s, contributing governments serviced civilian police operations on an ad hoc basis. Then – as now – the
supply of police officers was taken out of the pool of officers
budgeted to fulfil domestic needs in their home countries.[25] By
2001, this had become an untenable approach. Yet most contributing governments have been slow to accept and implement the
practical measures required to match the political and rhetorical
fervour with which they endorse the deployment of a large number of civilian police to conflict areas. Recent developments, however, might force governments into action. In 1999, it became clear
how serious staff shortages were when the UN almost simultaneously authorised operations in Kosovo and East Timor with
record-sized civilian police components.[26] The Brahimi Report
notes that 'as of 1 August 2000, 25 per cent of the 8,641 police
positions authorised for United Nations operations remained
vacant'.[27] The gaping hole in the supply of civpol staff is

exacerbated by frequent rotations that keep demand at a continuously high level.

Clearly, large civilian police contingents are here to stay and the need for police officers has to be built into domestic planning and budgeting. In addition to personnel resources, governments are increasingly called upon to provide funding for police training, equipment and institution-building – such as police academies and administrative structures – as part of efforts to re-establish or reform police forces in former conflict areas. Further, the stigma surrounding aid to internal security forces in developing countries is only gradually being overcome. With the international involvement in the Balkans, and to a slightly lesser extent in Latin America, the issue of transnational organised crime has also come to the fore. Western governments have 'welcomed' it as a justification for funds and other involvement, both out of real concern about the spread of organised crime but also as a potent tool in the face of public opinion which is sceptical about sending already scarce police resources abroad.

It is perhaps an uncomfortable reality that in the immediate future there will *not* be enough police officers. Creating a large enough pool of available officers would mean that domestic budgets would have to be increased substantially and new positions created in national police forces. Even if budgets and forces were increased – and there is no indication of this happening – there would be strong pressure from public opinion to deploy the additional policemen domestically. Contributing governments also have priorities for where they send officers and are particularly reluctant to provide policemen for dangerous missions, such as those that involve executive policing, for obvious reasons. This also applies to missions in the developing world that often draw the shortest straw when it comes to recruiting sufficient staff. Aside from the large peace operations in Namibia and Mozambique, there is a clear pattern of small police contingents in Africa, where the number of civilian police staff has been in the range of 30 to 250. The Brahimi Report triggered widespread criticism from the developing world that missions in Europe and the capacity being built up under EU auspices in the context of the Civilian Police

Initiative[28] might be at the expense of other poorer and less developed regions.

There is an obvious need for a sufficient number of policemen but there is a danger of getting lost in a futile debate over numbers. Instead – as is discussed in the following sections – pressure on recruiting an adequate quantity can be alleviated by improvements in the quality of staff, a better understanding of mission tasks and a more sophisticated approach to the types of skills required to fulfil these missions.

Getting Rid of the Dead Wood

A recurring problem for international civilian police has been their uneven quality. The issue of quality is two-fold. On the one hand, there are cultural, training and logistical differences between national contingents, as in any peacekeeping operation. Part of the value of multinational operations lies in the learning effect of cultural exchange. However, this is only true to the extent that it does not disable the mission. On the other hand, and far more damaging, some international police officers are simply not up to the job. Recruitment standards were first established in Cambodia (UNTAC), when the deployment of civilian police emerged as a standard element in peacekeeping operations, rather than an ad hoc measure. The three minimum requirements for international civilian police were defined as five years' police experience, the ability to operate a four-wheel-drive vehicle and the ability to speak the mission language, usually English or French.

There can be no doubt that low standards of policing by the international contingent can have a devastating effect on a peace operation. Perhaps the most severe consequence is a loss of credibility, respect and confidence among the indigenous police force and population. There has been the occasional case of misconduct among international police officers in most operations, Cambodia being a case in point. In addition to the lack of basic skills, some contingents were guilty of gross misbehaviour, such as abusing the local population, black-marketeering and running a prostitution business.

Yet the problem is not always as extensive as it at first appears: it only takes a few rotten apples to have a disastrous effect on a mission. In Bosnia-Herzegovina, for example, only 24 out of 10,000 officers that served in IPTF from 1996 to 2001 were repatriated for misconduct.[29] On the US side, the blame has been squarely placed on DynCorp, a defence contractor that the Department of State hired to handle all recruitment of United States' police personnel for international missions, which raises questions about how private security companies can be held accountable.[30]

Even when they are not involved in blatant misconduct, low quality staff are simply ineffective in their monitoring, training and policing efforts or, even worse, can spread bad practices by themselves disregarding democratic standards. Some officers come from countries where human rights are not respected in daily police practice and hence are inadequately prepared for international deployment. A final damaging effect is cost: repatriating unqualified international policemen is expensive and time-consuming, not to mention politically sensitive.

Attempts to ameliorate the problem – and costs – of low quality and staff repatriation were made in the mission to Bosnia-Herzegovina. Stricter guidelines and recruitment criteria were adopted and a civpol support unit was established in Zagreb that was later moved to Sarajevo. This unit tested new arrivals and provided a one-week orientation course. Although it brought some improvement, the one-week orientation could only provide a minimum of preparation. Additionally, given the pressure to recruit sufficient numbers, efforts to maintain a standard of quality control at times had to be diluted.[31]

Another problem is that quality is too often regarded only in terms of technical skills. Yet it has as much to do with the underlying attitude and values. A civilian police officer will find it difficult to pass on respect for professional policing, human rights and so forth to local counterparts when he does not represent these qualities himself in the course of his duty. A distinction has thus been made between minimum and maximum skills in the assessment of international civilian police. Minimum skills are the ones that emerged from the mission in Cambodia, i.e. driving and language skills. Maximum skills build on this base to require significant experience in different areas of policing. Experience provides a policeman both with technical skills, but more importantly with the flexibility and discretion to deal with the types of extraordinary situations that are common in a war-torn society. The ability to negotiate and other inter-personal skills are vital in international missions in which most incidents have a political dimension, concerns over personal safety are heightened and building a relationship with the community is critical. Specialised skills and training for missions are discussed in more detail in the next section.

Concrete measures have been taken at UN headquarters to address the issue of underqualified staff. UN CivPol has developed a screening programme run by 'Training Assistance Teams' (TATs), which pre-screen seconded policemen in their home countries. This measure has saved the UN both money and trouble, as unqualified contributions have been filtered out prior to deployment. In addition, UN CivPol encourages more pre-deployment training in donor countries. Courses that cover general peacekeeping training are the responsibility of, and usually conducted by, member states, i.e. the contributors. Pre-deployment training on the specifics of a given mission is conducted by the UN CivPol Unit.

Despite these laudable measures, problems of low quality persist, as reports from Kosovo and East Timor show.[32] One explanation is that control and enforcement mechanisms are not watertight. More importantly, there is considerable pressure to deploy rapidly and in large numbers, which means that officers cannot be tested or are accepted despite the fact that they do not meet the standards. In this respect, the issue of finding sufficient numbers of police staff is clearly connected to the question of quality. The greater the pressure to provide large numbers of police officers, the more likely that minimum standards will be set aside and, similarly, strictly enforcing the standards disqualifies a greater number of policemen and exacerbates the numbers pressure.

Another reason is internal UN politics. Experience has shown that police from non-democratic countries often do not measure up to the standards set by the UN CivPol Unit. To be fair, quality varies among the police officers from *all* countries – developed and developing – but a number of civilian police come from countries where human rights are routinely violated in daily law enforcement and police are corrupt and act as an instrument of state oppression. These officers are still accepted into missions due to the general shortage of available civilian policemen and – as is typical in the UN context – for political reasons, such as the desire to involve as many contributing nations as possible and to spread the burden of supplying police officers for peace operations. As long as the desire to appease some developing or non-democratic countries outweighs concern for deploying an effective and credible international civilian police force, peace operations will not be able to rid themselves of problems caused by unqualified staff.[33]

An obvious measure to counter civpol staff shortages is to delegate tasks to other participants in the mission. For instance, when monitoring human rights in police performance at later, more stable stages of a mission, the workload of civilian police might be relieved by deploying human rights monitors to replace some of the police officers. Examples of scaled-down monitoring missions in which human rights monitors have played a greater role are the UNPSG and the follow-on OSCE monitoring mission in Eastern Slavonia, the monitoring unit under United Nations Observer Mission in Angola (MONUA), and the proposals for a monitoring group to follow the planned withdrawal of the IPTF in Bosnia-Herzegovina in December 2002. The other cooperation partners that might relieve the international police are of course military peacekeepers. Military-police relations are discussed in more detail below in the section on cooperation within the mission.

The Need for Specialised Skills
A number of problems have arisen in the past, due to the fact that little attention has been paid to the particular background and prior professional experience of the international officers deployed. International policemen are often not experienced as monitors and teachers. Indeed, many officers may not have a talent for teaching – at home or abroad.[34] During UNTAES in Eastern Slavonia, there was a severe shortage of civilian police that had any experience as training staff. The subsequent UNPSG benefited from recruiting the best monitors from UNTAES, thereby improving institutional

memory and retaining experience.[35] Haiti is a counterexample, where 125 trainers were deployed with the mission.[36] Similarly, training local police in war-torn societies also addresses the role of police in a wider social context. This is not an issue that most international civilian police spend time considering in their home countries. There, most police officers spend their days solving particular crimes. In the mission, they are involved in shaping new public security systems and are required, although not accustomed to doing so, to thinking strategically about reform, its context and its consequences. In Bosnia-Herzegovina, for instance, the IPTF was adept at monitoring local police behaviour, but not all members of staff understood the implications of cooperation between the two Entities, the Federation and the Republika Srpska, and the need for a multi-ethnic composition in the Bosnian police force, the intricacies of democratic control, and so forth. Marotta underlines the importance of human rights training for civpol officers in firming up their understanding of fundamental principles. Her experience as a human rights trainer for the OHCHR has shown that all staff, regardless of nationality or origin, had a shaky knowledge of the role of human rights in policing and gained in confidence and credibility as a result of human rights training.[37]

In addition to formulating an overarching political vision for the long-term developments in a conflict area, contributing governments need to develop a better understanding of the competencies that are required to realise that vision. Decision-makers have been incapable of distinguishing between different types of units, such as between a monitoring unit and a professional training unit. Coupled with a lack of understanding of what a given mandate entails, low quality or 'mis-assigned' expertise has seriously undermined the effective execution of civpol missions.

Boutros Boutros-Ghali's much cited 'Agenda for Peace' of 1992 reflected the conceptual development that took place with respect to peacekeeping in the early 1990s. Similarly, a more sophisticated view of civilian police deployment is gradually emerging. Most importantly, the components and types of staff that a civilian police operation needs in order to fulfil its tasks is beginning to be better understood. In other words, thinking on civilian police staff for international missions has moved from 'a policeman is a policeman is a policeman' to thinking in terms of more specific job descriptions, such as traffic policemen, monitors, criminal investigators, trainers, or managers/administrators. In the past, the strengths and competencies of international policemen frequently went undetected, as most missions had no system by which to identify specific skills and match them to relevant tasks. Valuable experience also gets lost because of frequent rotations. Yet problems of quantity and quality can in part be alleviated by deploying police officers in accordance with their specialised skills. In recent operations, UN CivPol made an attempt to develop more specific job descriptions that would allow for a more focused, skill-specific recruitment of police officers. In Kosovo, the planners of the UN police mission took a first step in distinguishing between 'regular' civpol officers, specialised/formed police units, and border police.[38] UNMIK also established a Criminal Investigation Unit (CIU) which is located at KFOR Headquarters. In addition, trainers responsible for establishing the KPS were organised separately under OSCE auspices.

Nevertheless, putting the conceptual understanding into practice places much higher demands on how the UN requests staff from contributing governments; how staff are recruited and selected; and how the demands for staff in a mission are adjusted, communicated and met. Governments are sometimes also reluctant to provide their best officers, especially when it comes to personnel with scarce and expensive specialised skills, such as narcotics, organised crime, forensics, etc. More importantly, while commissioners and other managers in the field are beginning to identify needs more clearly, there are still significant communication problems between the field staff that conduct the actual hiring of personnel, contributing governments that supply the police officers, and UN headquarters. Until the late 1990s, all hiring of staff was processed through the UN in New York, wasting valuable time and effort and often not leading to any appointments at all, when applications disappeared into the UN's bureaucratic quagmire. Beginning with the missions in Kosovo and East Timor, field headquarters have been given greater authority to hire staff directly, creating a less circuitous link between supply and demand. But policemen still need to be seconded by their home governments and until the problems alluded to on the supply side are sorted out an efficient system remains out of reach.

The area in which most progress has been made with regard to matching in-theatre needs with particular specialised skills is the combating of organised crime. In 1999, for example, an Organised Crime Unit was established under the IPTF in Bosnia-Herzegovina.[39] The drive for improvements stems from an assessment, especially popular among European contributing governments, that an ability to deal with transnational organised crime and corruption is critical. In the Balkans, as well as in Central America, crime and corruption pose a major threat to the peace processes and are a source of instability – both internally and for the wider region.

It is sometimes overlooked – whether wilfully or not – that organised crime is the most difficult type of crime to fight, even in domestic settings. It requires a wide range of expertise, including a credible criminal intelligence network and an intimate knowledge of local culture and society. This reinforces the need for another specialised resource, namely an effective intelligence capacity. For example, it is quite clear that KFOR did not share intelligence with UNMIK.[39] Although civilian police can benefit from cooperating with the military in this area, one has to distinguish clearly between military intelligence and criminal intelligence, and between information needed to analyse patterns of crime and that required as evidence in a particular criminal case.

One suggestion that aims at ameliorating the potential problems caused by cultural differences takes its cue from the deployment patterns of formed police units, such as the French Gendarmerie, and proposes that civilian police be deployed in national contingents. That was the way in which the civilian police force was deployed initially in El Salvador, as the first and largest contributions came from a handful of 'friends of the peace process', including Spain, France and Italy. In Haiti, the Argentinean contingent was assigned responsibility for a specific geographic area. In both cases, there were a limited number of contributors, which facilitated policy coordination. It would be harder to do the same in Kosovo, for example, where 37 separate national units would each be practising their own brand of law and order while at the same time preaching the gospel of universal standards.

An alternative proposal to overcome the problem of cultural differences has been to assign specialised functions to a national contingent. For example, Norway could provide criminal investigators, Britain anti-terrorist or riot control experts, another country traffic policemen and yet another, trainers. This model is under discussion but has not been applied in any civilian police mission. Although it might appear functional, it requires planning for specific capacities, clear communication of needs and a level of political dedication from contributing governments that is at present utopian.

Training for International Deployment

There is considerable disagreement among practitioners, academics and other observers when it comes to the training of international civilian police staff. One line of argument claims that no training can prepare policemen for the reality of a mission and mission-specific conditions. Another runs that many of the challenges civilian police forces face can be alleviated by preparing officers for deployment with more comprehensive curricula and training courses. The middle ground is to improve the existing two-step approach.

The basic concept of the two-step approach is as follows: first, officers receive basic training on international deployment. As civilian police have become an established part of peace operations, the ideal would be if training became routine at national levels. The first phase of training could then be a standard element of police academy curricula, as police cadets come to expect a tour abroad as part of their police career. Currently, courses on international deployment are also held at a regional level, such as the cooperative venture among Scandinavian countries, but these efforts are still not comprehensive and differ widely between different regions of the world. UN CivPol's TAT programme does promote a standardisation of preparation but is far from covering all policemen deployed internationally.

The prime example of the lack of pre-deployment screening and training is the case of the United States. Although the US has been the largest single contributor, with more than 800 police officers deployed abroad in 2001, they are also the only country without a joint training programme. Instead, DynCorp, the private security company that recruits police officers for deployment abroad on behalf of the US State Department, conducts a nine-day pre-departure 'Police Assessment Selection and Pre-training Process' for the staff that it plans to hire. This is complemented by a brief, two-day introduction to conflict-resolution and negotiation at the United States Institute of Peace. Although the DynCorp process is intended as a thorough screening, during which officers with inadequate skills or profiles can be selected out, too many unqualified or unsuitable officers are still selected. The problem has been recognised by the State Department but little progress has been made in their efforts to coordinate training within the US. The situation also illustrates how bureaucracies, in this case the US State Department, have generally not made the necessary institutional arrangements for recruiting, selecting, training, deploying and debriefing police officers for international missions. In this way, domestic authorities are often the bottleneck that delays efforts to make civilian police operations more effective. It is critical that the responsible authorities in contributing countries take action to enable smoother and speedier recruitment and deployment, as well as better training for police officers.

In the second step of preparation, officers receive training on the specifics of a mission immediately prior to deployment or on arrival in the mission area. There is certainly room for improvement here, as many officers have an incomplete understanding of the scope of the civilian police contingent's mandate and of the circumstances in which the mandate is to be implemented. The OHCHR has provided in-theatre training in human rights in a series of missions, including ONUMOZ and most of the UN's Balkans missions. The courses were tailored to the specific context, taking into account the mandate and functions of the civilian police component, its relation to other parts of the mission and country-specific traits of the indigenous police forces. Courses ranged from one week in Mozambique to six months in Bosnia-Herzegovina and reached between a third and half of civpol officers.[40]

The issue of training is linked to the discussion of specialised skills above, in that a first step towards realising the potential in skills is to provide managers with more detailed training on the specific environment and their role in the mission. Given the high turnover rates that plague civilian police operations, a thorough preparation of managers ensures a consistent standard of abilities, which is essential. Although there is no doubt that training and mission-specific preparation can be improved, the understanding of an operation prior to actual deployment is often limited.

One option might therefore be to extend the present approach to a third step that would consist of calling in officers to a mission update after one or two months of deployment. This might be difficult to accomplish given the workload once in-theatre, which often makes on-site training impractical. However, it would provide a useful opportunity to adjust and standardise the approach of all civilian police, regardless of their organisational affiliation, throughout the mission area and among different national contingents. Most missions have followed a two-step pattern. Mozambique is one example where civilian police went through an induction programme and later received in-mission training on election monitoring and human rights. Yet the Mozambique example also illustrates the pitfalls in the process: the human rights course for this mission was delayed by four months as it was difficult to summon already deployed staff for additional in-theatre training.[41]

Weapons training and the question of armed versus unarmed missions was another aspect of training that initially triggered apprehension in some capitals. The primary concern for contributing governments was obviously the safety of their personnel. When the debate on whether or not civilian police should be armed first surfaced in the mid-1990s, there were no common testing standards or weapons training programmes. In the missions in Kosovo and East Timor, in which the international police were mandated to uphold law and order in unstable and crime-prone environments, carrying arms was considered a necessity. Weapons training and courses on the use of force were made standard parts of the induction training of UNMIK police.[42] As a result of the experience of those two cases, the debate on arming civilian police has been somewhat less tendentious. Most policemen do receive weapons training in their domestic settings as part of their police training and have enough discretion to know when to apply it. Again, problems associated with carrying arms link back to a thorough understanding of the mandate as a fundamental challenge for international civilian police deployment. The use of force in the absence of a clear vision of the role international police are expected to fill is very risky.

A Race Against Time or Chasing Windmills?

The early days of an operation are arguably the most critical. At this point the situation is still relatively fluid and a peacekeeping force, including its police component, has its greatest opportunity to influence the direction of events. This presupposes two elements: firstly, as we saw above, it is critical to have political agreement on a strategic vision of what is to be achieved by intervention. Secondly, it is essential to have the necessary means to begin implementing that vision. Delays in the deployment of a civilian police contingent have often been blamed for continued instability and a lack of progress in the early stages of peace operations. This is true in virtually all cases, ranging from Cambodia to Angola, Mozambique, Bosnia-Herzegovina and Kosovo. Clearly, the pace of deployment and planning are major challenges in civilian police operations.

Problems with rapid deployment flow naturally from recruiting an adequate number of qualified staff, as outlined above. The time lag between conception and implementation witnessed in many military peace operations is exacerbated for civilian police components, as it is difficult for contributing governments to free up scarce law enforcement capacity for international missions at short notice. Not least, because the pre-mission selection and training period takes longer for police officers than for peacekeeping soldiers.

The consequences of a delay in deployment will vary, depending on whether the international police are due to maintain law and order, i.e. conduct executive policing, or to monitor and train an existing and reasonably functional indigenous police force. Delays in the former case are more serious, since the international community will be expected to enforce the law from the outset of the mission. Paradoxically, it will also be more difficult to deploy rapidly to a level where the civilian police contingent has sufficient capacity to uphold the rule of law. For both monitoring and training and for executive missions, the UN CivPol Unit maintains that at least 9–12 months are needed to establish a police force with the necessary capabilities. Unless this is understood within the mission and among the local population, the police component's future leverage and credibility can be seriously undermined. The case of Mozambique illustrates a typical deployment pattern. The UN Security Council authorised ONUMOZ in Resolution 797 (1992) that was passed in December 1992, but had to await a formal request from the Mozambican government, which was issued in September 1993 – nine months later. The first substantial contingent of 278 civilian police observers was in place in April 1994, and the civpol component reached its full strength in autumn 1994. ONUMOZ was officially concluded in December 1994. A less extreme, but equally typical case is the IPTF in Bosnia-Herzegovina, which was authorised on 22 December 1995 but only reached approximately full strength in August 1996.

Efforts have been made to accelerate the pace of deployment. First and foremost, the UN and the EU are each discussing stand-by arrangements with rosters that would reduce the time needed for recruitment. Proposals have also been made to enhance intelligence gathering and fact-finding capacities in order to shorten response times and improve the basis for pre-mission planning. Intelligence gathering has long been a taboo topic in the UN, but the mood is beginning to change. The Brahimi Report, to the extent that it reflects changes in the UN's approach to peacekeeping, underlines the importance of intelligence and information. Although the lack of information-gathering capacity has been a major shortcoming of the United Nations system, decisions on whether or how to react to information are ultimately always political.

In truth, it has often been an unwillingness to act that has been the weak link in the chain. Both stand-by arrangements and improved intelligence-gathering capacity presuppose a shift in the stance of contributing governments. This would entail recognising that civilian police operations are an ongoing challenge rather than an ad hoc issue and translating this into domestic policy. This in turn means that national budgets and organisational structures should accommodate additional posts for staff deployed abroad at any given time and that national authorities should make it clear that they value the experience their police staff gain in a peace operation. In the past, an absence from the domestic beat has been a hindrance to the career of policemen that have been deployed internationally. Very few countries are moving in that direction or taking steps to facilitate the recruitment and deployment of personnel for international missions. One has to keep in mind that international deployment is and will remain a minuscule point on the agenda of a police organisation, which will always be centred on domestic crime fighting.

In short, improvements in the preparedness and response mechanisms of contributing governments and international organisations will be able to speed up deployment somewhat, but practical recruitment problems will remain, rendering instant deployment – as appears to be the aim – impossible in the near future. Instead, efforts should be made to optimise civilian police performance given the actual limitations on the ground. For instance, a system should be developed that identifies the competencies and capabilities that are needed first in a given conflict area. In most cases, this means accelerating the deployment of strategic resources, such as the mission head or police commissioner and key planning and preparation staff, or the establishment of police stations in clearly delineated areas that are particularly volatile. In that way, a civilian police operation can run as smoothly and effectively as possible, once policemen begin arriving in-theatre.

Planning is of course the essential precursor to deployment. The Cambodian case exemplifies the pivotal role of mission planning and how the lack thereof inhibited the execution of the civilian police operation. Preparations for what was to become the largest civpol element at that time only began with the appointment of a Civilian Police Commissioner in March 1992 – there was no provision for a civilian police component in the original mandate of November 1991. Deployment was relatively slow and 'planning and preparation for CIVPOL's deployment [in Cambodia] was virtually non-existent'.[43] In contrast, the UNPSG in Eastern Slavonia was operational from day one with regard to logistics and personnel, due to the transition planning that had taken place towards the end of UNTAES and the close cooperation between the two missions.

Implications of slow deployment will also be contingent on how the civilian police component cooperates with other parts of the mission. Lee and Metrikas underline that the lack of cooperation among different parts of UNTAC made starting conditions more difficult for the civilian police component: 'Lacking familiarity with the Cambodian situation and denied the opportunity to work together in developing common objectives and procedures for UNTAC, component heads were not able to engage in operational planning until the mission had already begun'.[44] Civpol wasted time by having to reinvent the wheel, which slowed down deployment of the civpol contingent and impaired its effectiveness. In the same way that staff shortages can be alleviated by better cooperation, the delegation of tasks at different stages of the mission among military peacekeepers, civilian staff, NGOs and the international policemen can lessen the effects of slow deployment. This is discussed in the following section.

Cooperation within the Mission

A realistic approach to civilian police deployment demands that one make the best of what is available rather than call for an ideal world in which resources are unlimited and there are no political aberrations. The discussion of the operational challenges has shown that some of the shortcomings of civilian police deployment have the potential to be crippling. In practice, however, the shortcomings are mitigated by cooperation within the mission, and this cooperation can be a determining factor in the effectiveness of international civilian police. The capacity to fulfil their tasks is greatly enhanced by the support of the military peacekeeping force, NGOs and other civilian staff. At the same time, civilian police are confronted with the needs and expectations of all their mission partners. For instance, the UNHCR in Kosovo was frustrated by the inability of the UNMIK police to provide security for returning refugees.[45] Whether or not that was part of the police mandate is to some degree irrelevant when these expectations exist and colour patterns of cooperation. Two central questions arise with regard to the division of labour: How can available resources be used in the most effective manner? And how can cooperation alleviate pressure on individual components of a mission, such as the civilian police?

Military–Police Cooperation

The performance of the international civilian police is most imme-diately affected by how much it can cooperate with the military. This is particularly true as operations have become more intrusive and occur in more unstable and criminalised conditions. In these conditions, the civilian police that never have, and do not aspire to, full area control can benefit hugely from military support, as a sort of force multiplier. The limited military–police cooperation that took place in the monitoring operations of the early 1990s con-sisted mainly of logistical support. With the expanding role of civilian police within peace operations, the interface between mili-tary and police staff has increased, providing more opportunities for, and placing greater demands on, their cooperation. By the turn of the century, military–police cooperation also included joint patrolling, military back-up, temporary use of military facilities for law enforcement purposes, such as for detention centres, and cooperation on criminal investigations.

While more opportunities for cooperation do exist, the recent expansion in this area points to the complexity and the limitations of military involvement in policing. It is important to keep in mind the wide differences in the various contributing countries in the culture and organisation of the military and the police and the ties between the two, as well as the challenges posed by diverging national interests, domestic policies and budgetary constraints.[46] This makes generalisations on the ability and suitability of the military in policing difficult, although some fundamental and conceptual issues are universally applicable. (The growing role of policing in peace operations and the increased overlap between military and police tasks has led to the introduction of formed police units that decision-makers believed would be the perfect hybrid and would be able to address gaps in military–police cooperation. The role of formed police units is discussed in detail in the following section).

The division of labour between the military and the police has been a source of debate throughout the history of civilian police contributions to peacekeeping. Civilian police are promoted as a welcome alternative to military forces quite simply because they are the cheaper and lower profile option for contributing governments.[47] With the emergence of public security issues as the key to stabilising a war-torn society and to consolidating a peace process, there has been a tendency to place an increasing share of the responsibility for maintaining security on the shoulders of civilian police. This has suited the military, which has never been keen to take on policing tasks. The instinctive rejection of policing tasks by the military, however, disregards the fact that forces have carried out policing in the past with military police and similar force units. The reluctance of the United States military to engage in policing was reinforced by the experiences in Somalia, despite the fact that UNITAF's limited assistance to the indigenous police force was one of the more successful aspects of the international intervention there.

With the operations in Kosovo and East Timor, attitudes among North American and European military staff have shifted slightly and there is a greater openness towards revising the division of labour. To some extent, the military have overcome their reluctance to be engaged in policing because to assist in resurrecting self-sustaining public security is increasingly seen as an effective and perhaps the only viable 'exit strategy'. This was stated as early as the operations in Haiti and Somalia and was gradually understood by SFOR and KFOR.[48] But there is also a danger of the opposite extreme, where military forces in their new-found eagerness assume policing tasks that they are not qualified for and can thereby undermine the fledgling rule of law. A differentiated and cohesive approach is called for.

In order to realise the potential of improved military–police cooperation two types of gaps in the provision of a stable environment have to be addressed.[49] The first type is a gap in deployment. The need for coordination between the military and the police is arguably the greatest in the pre-deployment and initial deployment phases. At this time, provision can be made to address challenges such as the gap between mission initiation and the deployment of the full civilian police contingent. This is also the time when the cohesive approach recommended in the discussion of the politics of mandates earlier in this chapter should be developed among the major contributors and not just between the military and the civilian police. At a more practical level, the military can alleviate public security concerns at the outset of an operation by providing equipment and other logistics support and conducting increased patrols, etc.

Military forces can also provide invaluable relief to civilian police forces and contribute to maintaining law and order even after the civilian police contingent has been fully deployed. For example, military patrols in the conflict area increase the visibility and credibility of the usually thinly stretched civilian police. In Bosnia-Herzegovina, the effectiveness of the IPTF was greatly enhanced when joint patrols with SFOR were introduced in 1997.[50] As a result of the closer association, the IPTF was regarded as a more credible actor by the local population and had the option of a more flexible and more immediate response to some of the tense situations that they encountered in the course of their monitoring activity.

The example of IPTF and SFOR cooperation already points to the second and more difficult gap to bridge, which is in enforcement. Where the moral authority of the civilian police is insufficient to ensure respect for or even enforce the law, military forces can contribute muscular back-up, engage in counter-terrorism efforts or assist in crowd control. Mandates now commonly call on the military to 'provide a secure environment' – both for international civilian staff and the local population. In Haiti, the Multinational Force was designed to create the stable conditions necessary for the deployment of UNMIH, which took over in spring 1995. Scholars and practitioners have underlined the critical role of the military in providing a deterrent to violence in both Haiti and Somalia.[51] The security situation in Kosovo and the executive authority assumed by NATO and the UN forced KFOR to include the maintenance of law and order in its mandate. However, the enforcement gap is very complex and can only be filled by developing so-called 'effective functional relationships'. In practice, Hills suggests that these relationships can be fostered and implemented through co-located headquarters, liaison procedures and officers, and via the development of compatible contingency plans and standard operating procedures.[52]

To date, there is virtually no evidence of a joint approach. Enhancing cohesion, especially through joint fact-finding and subsequent joint planning is critical, but such effort must still contend with two main stumbling blocks. Firstly, as was argued earlier in this chapter, military and police do not share a common conceptual or 'doctrinal' basis for their operations. In part, the military and the police simply do not speak the same language, but – prior to the advances in the large-scale missions of the Balkans and East Timor – civilian police operations were also long considered an add-on and subordinate activity to peacekeeping, as the case of Mozambique illustrates. Few funds were available for UN CivPol in ONUMOZ, and an expansion of the mission was only made possible when money was transferred from the military or ceasefire budget.[53] Although this view is gradually changing, the legacy that planning for an operation is exclusively military still dominates. This has contributed to delays in the deployment of civilian police and has resulted in poor cooperation between the military and the civilian police components in the early stages of a mission. In the Brahimi Report, specific measures were proposed to involve police officers in the military forces' pre-mission planning and fact-finding. It is as yet unclear how the proposals might be institutionalised.

Secondly, coordinated planning not only involves a clearly defined set of military and police planners, but stretches across several organisations and across different parts of the contributing domestic authorities. So far, it has proven very difficult to build practical contacts between all the decision-makers involved at national and international levels. Where there has been contact, too often it has been personalised and ad hoc. This is true of UN–NATO relations, as well as in relations with the EU and the OSCE.

In practice, the tendency to lump constituent tasks into two piles labelled 'military' and 'police' has proved unhelpful. The key to military–police relations is to develop a better understanding of

what exactly enforcing law and order in a foreign – and war-torn
– country entails. It is vital to achieve a sophisticated and flexible
distribution of labour in complex police operations. Cooperation
along the lines that emerged in Cambodia is a good example.
There, the military–police distinction was hazy with, for instance,
civpol providing a security presence at the polling stations during
the elections while the military peacekeepers secured the approaches to the sites.[54]

Since the civilian police began to play a greater role in the
early 1990s, there have been different organisational constellations
of military and police in peace operations. Initially, as in Namibia,
Mozambique or Angola and more recently in the UN operations in
the Democratic Republic of Congo (MONUC) and in Ethiopia and
Eritrea (UNMEE), missions were UN-authorised and led with a
very limited civilian police component. In Cambodia, Eastern
Slavonia and East Timor, military–police cooperation took place in
a wholly UN-operation, in which the civilian police component
played a substantial role. In these UN-only cases the lines of
authority within a mission were separate, where the civpol commissioner or a chief police officer reported directly to the SRSG on
a par with the commanding military officer.

Several cases have seen the involvement of other organisations or governments, in addition to the UN. Generally, the
responsibility for the police component has remained almost
exclusively in UN hands, but the military counterpart in an
operation has been provided by either NATO, as in Bosnia-
Herzegovina and Kosovo, or by coalitions of willing nations, as in
Haiti or Somalia. While the basic difficulties that emerge with
differences in culture, doctrine and organisation between the military and the police remain the same regardless of the authorising
organisation or constellation, practical difficulties can emerge in
terms of access to the operation's funds and resources, command
lines and competing authority in an area of operation. In Bosnia-
Herzegovina, the IPTF was the first UN police mission to operate
without an accompanying United Nations military force that
would normally have provided logistical support for the civilian
police contingent. As a result, IPTF experienced severe problems at
the outset of the mission.

In Kosovo, military and police planners addressed potential problems of competing authority by developing a flexible chain of command, which is similar to that established between the Royal Ulster Constabulary (RUC) and the British Forces in Northern Ireland. Authority moved from the military to the police commander and back, all in accordance with the level of tension in a given area and at a given time.[55] More generally, the cooperation between military and police varies with the intensity of the mission, especially with whether the civilian police component has an executive or a non-executive role. It also varies according to whether or not the military has an enforcement mandate and is authorised to 'use all necessary means', such as the MNF did in Haiti and UNOSOM II did in Somalia. If a web of 'functional relationships' emerges and the military–police dichotomy is diluted, primacy can become a problematic issue. Whether the military or the police take the lead in a given situation will have to be tested in practice. There is a fine balance between deriving benefits from flexibility and a differentiated division of labour and undermining hard-won cooperation and cohesion.

There can be no doubt that cooperation with the military has made civilian police work in peace operations more effective. However, there is a danger of assuming that good cooperation can provide all the answers to the conceptual and operational challenges of civilian police deployment. Therefore, it is imperative to take a closer look at the limitations and pitfalls of military–police cooperation. Firstly, when the military acts as a force multiplier for the police, the benefit of the 'deterrent' effect that the military undoubtedly has is not clear-cut. Although the civilian police gain in credibility by being able to call on a coercive threat, i.e. military back-up, the close association with a military force can also undermine public trust in a newly established or reformed rule of law. This is especially true in those countries in which the military has a history of being an instrument of oppression and domestic politics, such as in El Salvador or Haiti.

Secondly, there is a lack of mutual conceptual understanding. As was raised in the discussion of the conceptual basis for civilian policing above, this is in part due to a lack of common terminology. But more importantly, joint operations face fundamental problems when civilian police activity is marked by a glaring absence of doctrine and the military is guided religiously by its doctrine. In addition to these conceptual differences, the military and the police have different manners of operation, patterns of deployment and organisational structures. Whereas the military is composed of self-contained units, the civilian police component consists of individuals that are dependent on community support for communications, logistics and transport. Most of all, they differ in their approach to the use of force. Alice Hills regards this as the greatest obstacle for military involvement in policing. She points out that the military is the 'coercive resource of last resort' and argues that they cannot be seen to fail, in contrast to the police who rely on discretion and de-escalation of violence.[56]

Thirdly, the military simply does not know how to police and there is no need for them to learn. 'Providing a secure environment' is obviously a task that is akin to traditional peacekeeping and accepted military roles, but other tasks, the first and foremost of which is the investigation of crimes and the training of indigenous police forces, will have to remain in the hands of international police. There is no danger of the military drowning in a police role, as there are a host of jobs it simply cannot do. While it is clearly desirable that the military develop a greater understanding of the needs and modes of operation of the civilian police component, the military will not have to retrain or prepare to replace the civilian police in peace operations. It is also in the interest of the civilian police contingent that the credibility of the military as an effective muscular back-up is not diluted. As argued above, the key to improving military-police cooperation is identifying 'effective functional relationships' in which both sides support and complement each other without neglecting or undermining their own roles within the peace operation: for the military providing a secure environment and for the civilian police promoting the rule of law.

The Role of Formed Police Units

The role of formed police units, also called police with military status or Gendarmerie-type forces, is difficult to assess. The use of security forces with a role that falls somewhere in-between that of the military and the police is not new. But experiences with formed police units have been mixed and their role has evolved tremendously in the course of the 1990s. In 2001, observers were hailing police with military status as the panacea for many of the internal security issues that arise in the wake of conflicts. Assessments therefore tend to be anecdotal and tied to specific cases to an even greater extent than is true of civilian police. Formed police units are also difficult to assess, because their usefulness, effectiveness and credibility vary greatly with the nationality of each contingent. There is no such thing as the standard Gendarmerie-type force. Although they share a paramilitary character, each is trained, structured and deployed differently in accordance with domestic security needs in their home countries.

Early deployments took place in 1992–95, when contingents from the Spanish Guardia Civil and the Argentinian Gendarmeria Nacional were deployed in Haiti and El Salvador. In Haiti, the United States' Military Police and special forces worked closely with civilian police and the HNP on joint patrols and provided communication support at police stations.[57] In contrast to later deployments, these formed police units were integrated into the international police or military force without a separately defined function.

By the late 1990s, formed police units were regarded more as a strategic asset that was designed to fill a perceived gap between military capabilities and the abilities of unarmed police monitors. The first time a Multinational Specialised Unit (MSU) was created for this purpose was in Bosnia-Herzegovina in 1998.[58] The MSU was charged with the protection of returnees and elected officials, and could be called upon to assist in preserving public order *at the request* of the IPTF. The MSU in Bosnia-Herzegovina patrolled regularly, but by 2001 had 'only actually twice ... intervened in troubles'.[59] Nonetheless, experiences in Bosnia-Herzegovina were deemed satisfactory enough to convince decision-makers that an MSU in Kosovo would be essential to success. Indeed, planners in Kosovo created an MSU under KFOR command *and* a Special Police Unit (SPU), which is part of the UNMIK police structure and has a remit similar to that of the MSU.[60] The UN civilian police in East Timor also featured a Gendarmerie element, called the Rapid Response Unit, which consisted of 120 Portuguese and 120

Jordanian police with military status to deal with major security threats and large-scale emergencies.

Several problematic issues have emerged from the deployment of formed police units that should temper optimism about their usefulness. First, these units are as difficult to recruit as civilian police since they, too, usually form part of the daily public security structures in their home countries. Italy is perhaps the exception with its massive and intricate network of security forces, 120,000 of which are Carabinieri. The recruitment pressure has eased slightly as potential contributors have been made aware of the need for formed police units in peace operations and are coming forward with various forms of police with military status. However, some of these offers of troops pose further problems: as with civilian police, a number of these forces come from countries in which democratic standards are not upheld. Arguably this is a more serious problem for formed police units, as they are more heavily armed, play a more confrontational role and can therefore have a greater destabilising effect.

Second, there is the question of command lines and the degree of autonomy of the formed police units. The MSUs in Kosovo and Bosnia-Herzegovina were under military command and had the same rules of engagement (ROEs) as KFOR and SFOR respectively, but that did not mean that the two acted cohesively. Although in theory there is value in the flexible response option that the MSU provides, their role in practice is still somewhat unpredictable. In Kosovo, for example, their usefulness depended on how well the different unit commanders got along with their regional counterparts in KFOR. Alice Hills summarises the ambiguity that accompanies the deployment of MSUs in the following way:

> Gendarmes cannot replace military or police forces but only act in their support. Not only do gendarmes not remove the need for military involvement in extreme disorder but their introduction represents a militarisation of policing that may create more problems than it solves, sending the wrong signals in processes of reconciliation and democratisation. Their use also increases the likelihood of coordination problems between the various forces.[61]

This debate over lines of command and control is linked to the third issue, in that their autonomy, combined with national differences within the MSU and more importantly with the conceptual differences between the militarised police and civilian police, can lead to inconsistent and ineffective policing. Especially when training local police forces, it is highly disadvantageous when formed police units and civpol – who have to lead by example – are conducting two fundamentally different types of executive policing.[62] This problem was demonstrated, for example, in Kosovo, where the Italian Carabinieri dominated the MSU and introduced their own brand of policing. Although they have proved instrumental in the fight against organised crime, particularly smuggling and human trafficking, they have clashed with the UNMIK police on ethics and on matters of authority. The Carabinieri tend to act independently, as they do in Italy, and have been reluctant to submit to the law as it is enforced by the UN, thereby undermining cohesion and the promotion of one rule of law applicable to all.[63]

This pattern has been repeated elsewhere. In Somalia, the independence of the Italian Carabinieri and the French Gendarmerie undermined police training by introducing paramilitary elements. The same thing happened in Haiti, when the French Gendarmerie took over – under UNSMIH – from the earlier, more multinational UN effort and the focus of HNP training shifted away from community policing.[64] Similarly, according to one news report, the Portuguese formed police unit in East Timor did not prove to be very skilled at community relations, displaying macho, colonial-type behaviour and earning the description 'gorillas' from the East Timorese.[65]

Finally, when the MSU was first deployed in Bosnia-Herzegovina, its usefulness was hampered by the absence of a clear mandate, which prevented its capabilities from being fully exploited.[66] Although some progress has been made, the overlap between MSU and SPU functions in Kosovo indicates that neither NATO nor the UN have thought through what exactly the gap is that formed police units should fill. A better understanding of the strengths and weaknesses of each national contingent is essential to mapping out the role of a formed police unit.

Working with Civilian Staff and NGOs

Cooperation with civilian staff in peace operations is central for the civilian police. The most extreme cases are the operations in Kosovo and East Timor, where the international civilian police are an integral part of the UN civil administrations. Aside from any practical cooperation concerns, civilian police forces are dependent on political backing from the mission as a whole. This becomes especially clear with regard to civpol's monitoring activity, which depends on their moral clout. Being unarmed and only able to observe and to 'name and shame', they have no physical might in non-executive police operations. The Bosnian case underlines the value of a solid political backing. After Dayton's Year One there was a rush of critical reviews that triggered a re-evaluation of the agreement's provisions and its aims. This critical period lasted until spring 1997, when the international community – first and foremost the United States – reiterated its commitment to the agreement and thereby gave a boost to the authority of all the international implementers on the ground.

Similarly, in El Salvador pressure was also placed on the government to promote compliance with reform plans in 1992–95. The same course of action was chosen in Guatemala, but here pressure proved far less effective as the level of international commitment was much lower than in El Salvador and the approach less cohesive.[67] It would greatly benefit civilian police deployments if political backing for international civilian police were to progress so far that non-compliance by local counterparts in the field of law and order was considered worthy of sanctions and other political reprisals. This is not yet the case.

The civilian police component has extended support to other civilian staff in a variety of ways: providing security in the run-up to and during elections in Haiti, Mozambique, Cambodia, Bosnia-Herzegovina and elsewhere and assisting returning refugees in the Balkans, Cambodia and Mozambique. Other areas in which cooperation between the civilian police and other civilian staff is essential are human rights monitoring and the reform of the judicial and penal sectors. Moreover, threats to the security of humanitarian workers in conflict areas have increased steadily, with the result that military and police forces are often expected to provide protection, for instance, as occurred in Somalia. These additional demands, however, detract from the civilian police's ability to fulfil its mandate with regard to indigenous public security.[68]

Cooperation with human rights monitors is becoming steadily more important. In the early 1990s, human rights NGOs were still very sceptical towards any contacts with police assistance programmes, due to experiences with – mainly US – police assistance to Latin America in the 1960s and early 1970s and to the legacy of indigenous police forces as instruments of oppression.[69] It took five to ten years before the intimate link between the role of civilian police and that of human rights activists was acknowledged.[70] Non-police human rights monitors are commissioned by international organisations or work for NGOs and other self-appointed watchdogs, and are often active in monitoring courts, prisons and law enforcement agencies for their compliance with human rights standards. They also promote the development of indigenous civil society organisations to assume monitoring and oversight functions in the long run. A key cooperation partner has been the OHCHR, which has trained indigenous police as part of the 'UN Programme of Technical Cooperation in the Field of Human Rights'.[71]

More generally, the cooperation between civilian police and other human rights monitors points to the wider context of state-building and issues of governance. Cooperation between the two can facilitate the difficult transition from an immediate crisis management approach, i.e. providing a secure environment and policing, to long-term development assistance, i.e. state-building, democratisation, and economic development. The OHCHR and other human rights organisations often stay on after a peacekeeping or police mission has ended, as they did in El Salvador, where human rights projects have been conducted in cooperation with the government since 1997.[72]

There is a growing trend of authorising 'follow-on' missions, which in part are born out of the unwillingness of decision-makers at the UN – who are often major contributors to these operations – to authorise lengthy peacekeeping or police operations. Instead, conflict situations are addressed through a string of police missions that get progressively lighter as time goes by. The most important examples of this are Haiti and Eastern Slavonia. In Haiti, there was a near seamless transition from the IPMs to the first UN mission in Haiti – UNMIH. This was due to the fact that personnel and material requirements, as well as the concept of operation and the mission mandate had been worked out – in cooperation with the MNF – prior to deployment.[73] The amount of support provided by the international military force to UNMIH indicates that they considered the building of the basis for a viable civilian police component to be an effective exit strategy.

In Eastern Slavonia, the transition was made from a larger UN mission (UNTAES), in which the civilian police were but one element, to a follow-up mission, the United Nations Police Support Group (UNPSG) that focused entirely on matters of the rule of law. The trend should be welcomed as it provides continued international supervision and even more so demonstrates the commitment of the international community without being man-power-intensive operations. The trend towards consecutive police missions and longer-term involvement is reinforced by the rising awareness among donor governments of a wider reform agenda that emphasises the links between police reform, the judicial and penal sectors and democratisation efforts. At the same time, there is a danger that shorter mandates of a year or less undermine the credibility of international assistance. As Lake and Rothchild comment, 'external intervention that the warring parties fear will soon fade, may be worse than no intervention at all'.[74]

As a comprehensive approach to security sector reform is increasingly seen as essential, cooperation between the inter-national civilian police and staff involved in judicial and penal reform has also become more central. For civilian police forces, defunct judicial and penal systems mean that the efforts of the international as well as the indigenous police forces are discredited. Neither Cambodia, Haiti nor Somalia had functioning judicial systems. In Bosnia-Herzegovina – as in Kosovo and in most Central American cases – the absence of a functioning legal system was matched by rampant crime and a backlog of cases that had accumulated during the war. This increased the pressure on the indigenous police to make a visible difference quickly, while there was also a danger that the police force would become demoralised and public trust in the rule of law undermined when arrested criminals were released because the courts and the legal system were *unable* to try them. Exacerbating this problem further was the fact that often the courts were *unwilling* to try or convict criminals. Rachel Neild also points out how technical skills, such as collecting evidence and interviewing witnesses, are undermined when courts decide cases irrespective of its merits or evidence.[75]

In many cases, third-party efforts to reform the judicial system are dwarfed by the influence of the political framework that, to a large extent, determined day-to-day judicial activity. Although a 'court police' was established in Bosnia-Herzegovina to provide protection for judges and prosecutors and the IPTF monitored court activity, it proved difficult to combat the intimidation of staff and plaintiffs.[76] In Kosovo, the UN felt the pressure even more keenly since the international civilian administration itself was responsible for investigation, arrest, detention and trial of criminals, rather than monitoring a local, if flawed, system of law and order. The scope of the challenges of security sector reform and particularly its political dimensions underline the point that unless these efforts form part of a cohesive approach and enjoy staunch political backing, they will ultimately prove futile.

Chapter 3

Dealing with Crime and Political Recalcitrance

The context in which international police must fulfil their mandate is critically important but is often neglected. Time and again, action plans are drawn up without detailed knowledge of the context of their implementation. And invariably, damning criticism of civilian police is made without consideration of the circumstances of their deployment. The most important aspects of the mission area that shape the context for civilian police deployment are the level of crime and instability and the degree of cooperativeness of political authorities and other power holders. The situation in Haiti in 2001 is an example of how the progress achieved through extended police assistance is nullified by a continued political stalemate. These destructive influences must be marginalised in order for civpol operations to ultimately be successful.

Clearly, crime and criminal networks constitute a policing problem for both the international and the local civilian police. In turn, crime is closely tied to the political context, as political leaders are often involved in criminal networks and vice versa. Therefore, the third section of this chapter points to the need to strengthen local police capacity to address the challenges of crime and corruption and to build popular confidence in a system of law and order that is democratically accountable.

People and Politics – Local Support for Civilian Police

The influence of external efforts to enhance public security in war-torn societies pales in comparison to the local circumstances in which the international mission is deployed. Political *and* popular support are essential for creating a self-sustaining system of law and order, elements of which are considered below. There is the traditional concept of consent that applies to civilian police as much as to peacekeepers. There are legal questions on the right to intervene and on the applicable criminal code. There is the need to manage popular expectations. And, most importantly, there is the difficulty of identifying whom best to work with and of balancing the interests of local counterparts against those of the international civilian police mission. For instance, it is far from certain that political leaders that have used local police forces to consolidate their power in the past will find it easy to work with an independent police force and judiciary, or that corrupt police officers are willing to curb their own power and income by submitting to performance reviews. These are examples of the interests of local counterparts that international civilian police have to be aware of when attempting to reform, monitor or train local police forces.

The Political Context of Civilian Police Missions

It is important to grasp just how momentous the development towards more intrusive missions has been. After all, meddling with the indigenous police goes to the heart of a state's sovereignty and its monopoly on coercive means. In order to minimise concerns about external actors challenging local sovereignty, the organisations that deploy civilian police have been careful to establish a sound legal basis for each intervention. A Memorandum of Understanding (MoU), a binding document that outlines rights and obligations of each party, is signed between the host government and the international civilian police. As we have seen above, the scope of a mandate only really emerges in its implementation. Similarly, Halvor Hartz, former head of UN CivPol in New York, points out that the value of the MoU can be variable. He cautions that relying on an MoU presupposes that there is an effective government or authority that will be able to supply the goods.[1] In Somalia, Mohammad Farah Aideed and other faction leaders did not accept the authority of the SC Resolution and therefore did not cooperate with the UN operations.[2] In any case, the standard MoU is adjusted to local circumstances in the course of the mission through additional agreements on particular issues that are usually negotiated by the UN.

The existence of a criminal code or constitution, or both, also forms part of the legal context. The Brahimi Report points to the difficult legal basis of a UN engagement in civil administration, such as in Kosovo and East Timor, when it assumes responsibility for maintaining law and order. The absence of a legal footing for the implementation of executive authority is a key problem. The report suggests the development of an interim UN criminal code that would reflect basic human rights and some standard criminal laws.[3] At the time of writing, this proposal is under discussion but no further progress has been made. A particularly tricky question in the wake of civil conflicts is whether a legal code exists and if it does, how useful – how tainted or how practical – it is. In the context of police reform, the existence of an applicable legal code is critical in that it guides international police officers in those cases where they have to enforce law and order, such as in Kosovo and East Timor. It is also a necessary precondition for training or reforming indigenous police forces. To the population in a war-torn society, the absence of a generally accepted and enforced legal code indicates instability and inconsistency and does little to encourage faith in the rule of law.

One of the most difficult decisions for outsiders, such as the UN, is determining who constitutes the real authority. More often than not, governments in conflict-ridden societies have lost control over the use of coercion and legal violence. In a war-torn society, the state's monopoly is frequently challenged by alternative security arrangements, such as opposing armed forces in El Salvador, Cambodia and Mozambique, specialised police forces in Angola and Bosnia-Herzegovina, or other paramilitary groups, including the KLA in Kosovo or the Albanian clan structures. As noted above, the security vacuum will never be complete – and certainly not lasting. If the state is unable to fill the vacuum, alternative non-state security providers, such as insurgent vigilante groups, will crop up. International efforts to reform indigenous police forces therefore aim at resurrecting the government's security apparatus. At the same time, assistance aims to ensure that government security forces and their conduct conform to democratic standards. The international civilian police's ability to conduct executive policing is also impaired where civilian police forces have to compete with an existing local but biased or dysfunctional police force for final authority. In Cambodia, the unwillingness of the political authorities to accept the UN's civilian police as a player in public security and a guarantor of law and order blocked its access to judicial institutions and undermined its authority and effectiveness.

The distribution of power in most immediate post-conflict situations is often hazy in that the leaderships in the political, military, economic and criminal spheres are intertwined and often one and the same. By selecting and empowering a certain group of people as local partners, one may end up either dealing with an ineffectual leadership that lacks popular support, or inadvertently legitimising criminal networks. Both cases were in evidence in the Balkans. In elections in Bosnia-Herzegovina, the promotion of obscure moderate candidates that were international favourites was not very successful, because the candidates lacked popular support and were regarded as international lackeys that did not represent the people of Bosnia. At the other end of the spectrum, KFOR and the UN tacitly accepted the KLA's claim to formal political power when they allowed the occupation of town halls throughout Kosovo by the KLA in the immediate aftermath of NATO's bombing campaign. In addition, spoilers emerge from among local counterparts in virtually all peace processes. Spoilers have more to gain from maintaining instability and are therefore opposed to the deployment of international civilian police and, more importantly, opposed to a restructuring of their own police forces. In El Salvador, both the military and political leadership were loath to relinquish control over the police and as a result, were highly uncooperative. In contrast, during the deployment of the United Nations Police Support Group (UNPSG) in Eastern Slavonia, the fact that the Croatian government proved supportive and cooperated closely with the mission was a major contributing factor to the achievements of the UNPSG. Thus, the degree of cooperativeness has implications for the effectiveness of civilian police operations.

Moreover, there is a clear need for a 'national political will' to support police reform efforts. In other words, the institutional framework has to reflect and support democratic policing practices. This is true of the political authorities, but there also needs to be room for input from civil society groups and professional organisations, so-called reform constituencies.[4] The international police missions in Haiti worked with the Haitian government to set up an HNP Development Plan until 2000, the implementation of which was then overseen by a Support Group that included local and international representatives.[5] Although the term 'ownership' has become far too common, it nonetheless has value with regard to designing a sustainable indigenous public security network. A vision cannot be entirely imposed from the outside. Instead, local authorities must have a say in the model of police force and the wider law and order framework that is being established, or it will lack political support and will not be sustainable. Arguably, the fact that the High Representative made laws in Bosnia-Herzegovina on a doubtful legal footing did not increase public confidence in the Bosnian legal system that the UN helped establish.[6]

In contrast, the Somali case was – for a time – a 'showcase' for involving local community leaders and thereby for sustainability and empowerment. When the Auxiliary Security Force (ASF) was set up, much of the decision-making on the future form and function of the Somali police was left to local dynamics. Somali warlords, including the two dominant factions of Aideed and Ali Mahdi, established an apolitical police committee consisting of professional police and a few political appointments. The latter were outnumbered and thereby effectively neutralised in the committee by the police representatives and the international observers, who were more interested in professionalising the Somali police than in continuing the political struggle. The police committee formed a central and effective contact point for international police efforts. However, the ASF was later challenged by the warlords, who were intent on escalating the civil war. One can speculate that this was a necessary move on their part because the ASF began to function too effectively and to threaten their power. The lesson drawn from this case is that, ultimately, the ASF could not be made to work in the absence of a political resolution of the conflict. Underlining the need for a beneficial political context, Thomas and Spataro believed that 'inability of the Somalis to come together in any sort of peaceful consensus' destroyed all hope of creating an effective, democratic police force.[7]

Managing Popular Expectations

In addition to juggling the interests of politicians and other power holders in economic or criminal spheres, the international civilian police force also has to develop good relations with the population at large. More specifically, this entails managing people's expectations – predominantly those of the local population in a conflict area – of the international operation and of their own indigenous police force.

A good rapport with the local population is essential to effective civilian policing, as officers are far more intimately tied to the community than a military force is. Although they arrive as national contingents, civilian police are assigned as individuals. They must also find and pay for their own housing. In other words, good community relations and confidence in local and international police forces lays the basis for effective policing, be it monitoring or executive policing. As Hartz put it, 'policing is not only a 'technical' profession: more importantly, it is a moral profession, requiring the confidence of those it serves in order to be effective'.[8] Neild even argues that public cooperation was more important than technical skills for the HNP in Haiti. There, however, the efforts of the civilian police to gain the confidence of those they served was hampered by their inability to speak the local or the mission language; this problem was further exacerbated by a shortage of interpreters.[9] The absence of close ties makes the civilian police's – and the local police's – efforts ineffective and unsustainable.

The need to manage popular expectations appears obvious, but is seldom ranked as a high priority in a police operation. Indeed, the UN has a well-deserved reputation for being weak on public relations. This reputation is the result of operations such as UNTAG, where people did not know who the civilian police deployed throughout Namibia were or why they were there. In part, managing expectations simply means explaining the why, who and how of an international operation. This was managed well in Haiti, for example, where Military Information Support Teams (MIST) were deployed for this purpose and simultaneously served as a contact point for the Haitian government.[10] However, in societies that have been subject to propaganda and misinformation, communicating an understanding of the civilian police's tasks and limitations is difficult.

The series of operations in Somalia also illustrates the importance of managing expectations and the detrimental effect on credibility when this fails. To begin with, UNOSOM I had been completely ineffective. Then, expectations were built up with the Auxiliary Security Force (ASF) during UNITAF when serious effort was put into professionalising the Somali police, not only through training, but through assisting the Somalis in trying to build a political consensus on the rule of law. But then public security was given a lower priority in the UN's follow-on mission UNOSOM II, which began in May 1993, and the ASF was abandoned again. This last step precipitated major disappointment over the international efforts to provide security to the extent that the local population was merely waiting for the withdrawal of the international mission so that they could make their own public security arrangements.[11]

The experience in Somalia also shows that in their relations with the local population the credibility of the international civilian police depends on their actual performance, i.e. their ability to police, to provide security and, in some cases, also on their ability to bring about visible change. In this respect, Liaison Agreements – i.e. stipulations on the conditions of deployment and cooperation with local counterparts, along with the geographic spread of the force and its density – affect how civilian police are perceived and how accessible the international police officers are for the local public.[12]

One problem for civilian police, especially when carrying out more limited monitoring mandates, is dealing with the exaggerated expectations of the indigenous population. This is especially true when the international policemen are themselves uncertain about their roles and are insufficiently aware of the 'hands off' approach inherent to a monitoring mandate, i.e. to observe but not to enforce law. This inadequate briefing has resulted, for example, in civpol 'dabbling' in executive policing in missions in Cambodia, Haiti and Somalia without actually being asked to do so in the original mandate. A further problem arises from the fact that the intricacies of the international approach and the distribution of responsibility among various international organisations are often lost on the locals. As Schmidl points out, 'for the people on the ground, security is indivisible'.[13]

A case in point is the criticism directed at the International Police Task Force in Bosnia-Herzegovina in connection with the flight of Bosnian Serbs from the Sarajevo suburbs. Unrealistically, IFOR passed on the responsibility for providing an effective security guarantee and reassuring scared Bosnian Serbs on to the civilian police monitors. At the time, in February 1996 – shortly after the Dayton Agreement – only 230 unarmed monitors had been deployed; the IPTF was not yet functional and enforcing the law was not part of the mandate of the police monitors. This was not made clear to either the Bosnian population, which looked forward to the deployment of an objective police force to keep them safe, or to international onlookers, who immediately seized upon the inability to prevent the exodus of Serbs from Sarajevo as an example of yet another UN failure. Arguably, it took the IPTF almost a year to recover from its inability to live up to exaggerated expectations and made it more difficult to gain popular confidence.[14] It also served as one of the first eye-openers for IFOR, which realised that handing over responsibility for such 'civilian tasks' on to the IPTF was not a tenable approach and that closer military–police cooperation was necessary.

Similarly, Mozambicans expected the civilian police contingent of ONUMOZ to guarantee the human rights of the population and provide public security. They had no conception of the limitations of civpol's monitoring role.[15] Cambodia is an example of the worst case, in which disappointed expectations led to outright hostilities and 'in the period leading up to the elections, a campaign of violence directed at UNTAC civilian and military staff and UN volunteers'.[16]

In line with the increasing intrusiveness of UN operations and the changed attitude towards sovereignty, civilian police, as

well as virtually all other international staff, have lost their reputation of impartiality which was a pillar of UN peace missions
during the Cold War. As a result, the rationale for a hands-off
advisory role that derives its power from its moral authority has
also been weakened. Therefore, it has been more difficult for
unarmed monitors to assert their authority in more recent operations. The loss of impartiality is particularly problematic in executive policing operations: the more intrusive the activities of
international police have become, i.e. the more they have moved
from simply monitoring or observing to maintaining law and
order, the more difficult it has become for the civilian police to
remain impartial. More importantly, as impartiality is above all a
matter of perception, the more assertive the civilian police act, the
more they risk affronting one of the parties to the conflict and the
more likely the local population is to view them as partial. The
difficulty inherent in assuming full responsibility for public security becomes clear in the International Crisis Group's assessment of
the UN police's performance in Kosovo. Although 'a climate of
lawlessness and disrespect for the institutions of public order'
could be the product of any number of factors, it 'is perceived by
most Kosovars as the greatest institutional and public policy failure
of the international mission'.[17]

UNMIK and OSCE staff involved in policing and police
training in Kosovo argued that priorities were largely defined by
the local population. In order to enhance the accessibility of the
UNMIK police, the police tried to be visible and establish credibility early on. An increase in the number of complaints submitted
to UNMIK indicated that the local population's trust in the international police had also increased. In El Salvador, Haiti and
Guatemala, reform efforts also led to greater popular confidence, as
the new public security forces were considered an improvement
and were welcomed by the population. However, as the example
of Haiti shows, trust was fragile and eroded rapidly when the HNP
was considered ineffective. The population reverted back to
alternative security providers, including 'popular justice' and private security firms, in their frustration.[18]

Reforming a police force, therefore, also entails shaping local
expectations on what to expect from the reformed police. For the

principle of accountability to make sense and to be a check on police conduct, the local population has to care enough to demand that local police live up to certain standards. This refers to expectations of both individual members of society and of civil society organisations and other reform constituencies. Civic education programmes often aim at developing a better understanding of the role of police forces in society, including the role of the international police, and of the rights and responsibilities of community members. In this area, civilian police forces have to work closely with those NGOs engaged in civil society development and democratisation programmes.

Violence and Crime in War-torn Societies

The preceding section has argued that popular expectations and popular confidence are critical factors in the effectiveness of civilian police operations. It also argued that the population in a war-torn society looks to the international and the local police to bring about visible change. Perhaps the most tangible measure of improvement – and thereby a measure of whether or not to trust in the rule of law – is a reduction in violence and crime.

Many war-torn societies experience a surge in crime in the wake of a conflict, so that the level of crime in-theatre is often higher than in 'normal' societies.[19] Mozambique, for instance, was virtually crime-free during the war, but became engulfed in a wave of lawlessness when the conflict ended.[20] Besides being a challenge for indigenous police forces, high crime rates are extremely de-stabilising in a fragile 'post-conflict' state where the population's concern for their security is already heightened. In the case of the Balkans, European governments are concerned about containing or fighting crime to keep it away from their own doorsteps. More fundamentally, crime needs to be fought because everyone has the right to live in relative safety. Furthermore, scarce economic resources are tied up in criminal activity and need to be re-directed to promote economic reconstruction that benefits all and removes financial incentives for continued instability.

When external actors assist in re-establishing law and order, they are faced with a concept of law and order that might be different from that in 'normal' peaceful societies.[21] Rather than aim at a crime-free society, which is unattainable even in the most developed of Western societies, a more realistic measure of success might be to arrive at 'tolerable' levels of violence and crime.[22] Obviously, as long as crime has a destabilising effect on Kosovo, as well as on other war-torn countries, it must be fought. Nevertheless, expectations are at times unrealistically high.

If local authorities cannot effectively cope with internal security challenges, persistently high crime rates also threaten to reverse progress in reform. James Woods describes how the Mozambican population gradually lost faith in the local police with the result that the police became marginalised – which in turn did not inspire confidence among the people. As a result, the police resorted to excessive force and the population increasingly took the law into its own hands.[23] This problem was also widespread in Haiti.

In most cases where crime continued unabated, such as Mozambique, Haiti and El Salvador, the credibility of the police decreased at the same time as popular pressure on the government to provide public safety rose. When crime was not brought under some form of control, popular demand even encouraged the use of repressive measures by local authorities, undermining reform and democratisation efforts.[24] In a volatile situation, the separation of military and police forces is one of the first achievements to be threatened. In the El Salvadorian case, the government and military deemed it necessary to deploy armed forces along national highways in order to combat the rise in crime.[25] Obviously, reintroducing the military into law and order functions sets a dangerous precedent and undermines the credibility of the local police. Furthermore, when international civilian police become involved in reforming local police forces they are not spared local criticism. For example, when the HNP proved less effective than had been hoped, Haitians blamed international intervention for worsening the situation.[26]

In addition to high crime rates, politically motivated violence is often prevalent. However, it should be noted that any crime is likely to be interpreted in the light of the recent conflict. Even more so, criminals often need political cover to operate effectively. This adds a political dimension to law enforcement that makes policing a highly sensitive activity, which international civilian police do not usually have to deal with in their home countries. It also means that government measures to combat crime might be interpreted as aggressive acts and a continuation of the conflict. In short, if *not* dealt with, crime is highly destabilising; if dealt with, it is a potential minefield.

With slight modifications, a description of the Balkans fits most cases in which civilian police have been deployed. There, the surge in crime was a response to the break-up of Yugoslavia in the early 1990s – the collapse of the communist state and the resulting void left by an ineffective security apparatus or a corrupt police. This left an opening for opportunists and entrepreneurs in the criminal realm, who built strong informal networks both inside and outside the region. The situation was exacerbated by the lack of other employment opportunities and the wave of demobilised soldiers and police officers that washed over an already depressed labour market. In part, however, what appeared as a surge in the crime rate was in truth the continuation of a war economy that mutated into and became visible as black market activity. Black market activity in turn clearly thrived on both the absence of effective authority and progress in economic reconstruction.

Combating Different Types of Crime

There are roughly four types of crime that international and local civilian police face in a war-torn society. Firstly, there is ethnically or politically motivated harassment, which, as has been pointed out above, amounts to and is perceived as a continuation of the conflict. Crime may also result from unmet or unsatisfied grievances that are left over from the conflict. These will in most cases be expressed through ethnically or politically motivated crime. In Bosnia-Herzegovina, little thought was given to the ethnic divisions in the design of the Dayton Agreement and to the fact that the protection of ethnic minorities would be non-existent. Both in Kosovo and Bosnia-Herzegovina harassment has been widespread. An OSCE report on patterns of violence in Kosovo described the violence as systematic, where victims were often carefully targeted and former KLA members were behind it.[27] When violence is organised, systematic and motivated by political

Table 1 Types of Crime in War-torn Societies

Manner of organisation		
Motivation	Individuals	Groups
Political	1. Politically or ethnically motivated	2. Terrorism/ insurgency
Non-political	3. 'Petty' crime	4. (Transnational) Organised Crime

objectives, it can be described as terrorism[28] and insurgency – the second type of crime – and can in the worst case lead to a resumption of full-scale hostilities.

Thirdly, there is petty – but still violent – crime, including muggings, kidnappings, or rape. This type of crime is either committed by opportunists – this was clearly the case in Guatemala, Haiti, El Salvador, and Mozambique – or occurs as a side-effect of politically motivated or organised crime. Finally, the type of crime that has preoccupied some governments contributing staff for international police missions is organised crime. In most cases, organised crime will be transnational, as in the Balkans, the area of the former Soviet Union, or Colombia and attempts to tackle it have to be regional and long-term. Most war-torn societies are afflicted by all types of crime to varying degrees and the distinction between the different types can be blurred. This is especially true with regard to distinguishing between terrorists and organised criminals. The two types are closely linked, when terrorist groups finance their activity through organised crime and organised criminals frequently wield significant political influence, even if not in any official capacity. In practice, ideology and financial interests are not as distinct as they may at first seem.

A major shortcoming of international efforts to establish the rule of law has been the reluctance to deal with informal networks of power. These networks are difficult to identify and usually retreat into the shadows when the sometimes boisterous international organisations arrive, as they did in Kosovo, pre-occupied with internal operational issues and kicking up dust in an attempt to get the mission off the ground. Although they become less visible, these networks continue to control and manipulate political and economic structures, as well as people, and are no less influential. The three ethnic groups in Bosnia-Herzegovina established informal parallel lines of authority within the police despite the official restructuring of the Bosnian police forces into multiethnic units. Each informal parallel police organisation was responsive mainly to the members of its particular ethnic group and commanded various irregular paramilitary back-ups, undermining the impartial application of the law. In the context of police reform, removing parallel command lines and increasing the responsiveness and accountability of the local police forces is critical to developing popular confidence in the rule of law.[29] In Haiti, criminal networks and 'unofficial' political groups increased and exploited the reigning insecurity and seriously undermined progress in the field of public security.[30] Few efforts were made to draw informal networks into the state-building project to enhance popular support and create a more viable system. Obviously, there is a fine balance between incorporating informal actors into reform projects and marginalising counterparts that are unacceptable. Differentiation in these cases is vital as most informal networks coincide with criminal structures. Allowing groups to operate that derive financial benefit and curry political favour through instability and tension means, to put it bluntly, selling out the peace process.

Although individual measures, such as anti-corruption programmes, were initiated in both Bosnia-Herzegovina and Kosovo, there was no cohesive political approach to the issue of informal networks, criminal or otherwise. A first step might simply be to take more consolidated action against the politically motivated violence that accounted for instability and the lack of progress in minority returns, as well as for continued displacement.[31] Consistency is lacking when it comes to a coordinated approach, both among military and civilian actors, including the police, and among individual contributing nations, such as between European countries and the United States.[32] In most cases, there was a vast amount of intelligence on informal networks, but networks are also extremely difficult to deal with. For a start, essential political support from local authorities is usually absent as they fear losing their grip on power. More importantly, the international community is at a loss as to *how* the influence of informal actors can be curbed.

Informal networks are sometimes rival 'security providers' and in the cases of Kosovo and Cambodia, where the Khmer Rouge retained much of its military might, were a continued threat to stability.[33] With no other employment options, private security firms or criminal gangs offer attractive career opportunities. In addition, as John Cockell points out, 'the popular association of the KPC with the legacy of the UCK [KLA] has also tended to undermine the position of the KPS as the only legitimate indigenous, uniformed law enforcement agency in Kosovo'.[34]

A fifth type of violence that might be added arises when the external forces become direct targets of violence or sabotage. As the mission in Cambodia began to deploy and make their presence felt throughout the country, violence against UNTAC personnel and helicopters increased.[35] In August 2001, the death of Sapper Collins during the first days of Operation Essential Harvest in Macedonia provided another reminder that international interventions are not always greeted with unmitigated enthusiasm. In Kosovo and Angola too, the international presence lost its status as a sacrosanct entity and was subject to attacks of varying intensity, from throwing rocks to shooting down planes.

The level of violence and types of crime also give some indication of the capabilities that both indigenous and international police forces need. This leads us straight to a discussion on the establishment or reform and restructuring of indigenous police forces.

Creating a Democratic Police Force

The basic activities of police reform were outlined in Chapter 1 above. But as creating a sustainable democratic police force is the only realistic way of allowing the civilian police to conclude their mission and claim success, reforming and restructuring indigenous police forces warrants a closer look. Strengthening this capacity is also the most pronounced activity in international police operations, in the sense that civilian police spend the most effort and donors spend the most money on training and subsequently monitoring indigenous police forces. In essence, the assignment is to transform a police force that fits some or all of the following descriptions: under military or political control, ineffective, corrupt, disrespectful of human rights and ethnically divided. The 'ideal' result of the transformation, Call and Barnett suggest, are 'civilian, apolitical police forces that are composed of different political contingents and ethnic groups, and who will protect citizens, uphold the rule of law and help to maintain order with a minimum of force'.[36] The question for civilian police and the other international actors involved in the public security field is how to guide the transition and how to accelerate the process of transition.

It would be an exaggeration to claim that the host of international actors involved in providing police assistance have developed a common approach to police reform. Nevertheless, one can identify a few key concepts, such as democratic policing, community policing, and perhaps the more value-neutral concept of professionalisation. *Democratic* policing has two essential features: responsiveness and accountability. As David Bayley writes, a 'police force is democratic when it responds to the needs of individuals and private groups as well as the needs of the government ... and [is] accountable to multiple external audiences'.[37] The concept of *community* policing underlines the need for responsiveness and – as the name suggests – close ties to the community. When international assistance emphasises the *professionalisation* of the police force as a key aim, it clothes normative concerns in terms of effectiveness and social value and renders them less politically sensitive.[38]

Reform efforts follow a two-pronged approach. First, police reform involves a structural component. This refers to questions of basic restructuring, such as the multi-ethnicity of indigenous police forces, sustainable force levels and salary structures. In order to be sustainable in the long run, structural reform must also build an institutional framework – including administrative structures – as well as links to governing institutions and to the other elements of the public security field.[39] Second, structural reform is an empty shell unless police behaviour also changes and the police abide by democratic standards.

Restructuring Indigenous Police Forces

The UN efforts in Bosnia-Herzegovina are a good example of structural reform. There, the police force was bloated in the aftermath of the war and had actively participated in the conflict.[40] As a result, structural reform required three actions: reduction, reorganisation, i.e. separating military and police forces, and vetting. First, the police force, which had swelled to 54,000, had to be reduced to 20,000. This also meant dismantling special police forces and similar armed groups. Reductions were necessary simply to arrive at sustainable force levels and salary structures that the Bosnian governments in the two Entities would be able to finance without outside assistance in the long run. The process of reduction however, was also a convenient filter whereby police officers were screened in a systematic vetting procedure. The process continued for more than five years and developed a corollary, decertification, which was used to punish unacceptable behaviour. Decertification proved a useful enforcement mechanism to back up monitoring activity. Although the vetting and certification process has been criticised for taking a long time – and had made little progress by 1999, the IPTF argues that it will ultimately be all the more stable. Whereas vetting is initially a structural technical process, it becomes an issue of police behaviour in that officers that disrespect human rights can be purged from the force. Similarly, the OSCE and UNMIK police reserved the right to dismiss KPS officers for up to three years after they begin field training. In that way, vetting is a true test of reform in the long run.

The third action in structural reform is a reorganisation and more particularly the separation of military and police forces. In both Kosovo and Eastern Slavonia, the new police forces were to be kept separate from the influence and participation of paramilitary forces, such as specialised police forces and other armed groups of different shapes and affiliations. In Kosovo, this meant disarming and removing the influence of the KLA to the greatest extent possible.[41]

A different approach was chosen in Haiti. Despite the fact that the FAd'H performed both military and policing duties and were heavily politically influenced, there was no choice but to use some of the FAd'H as the core of the new purely civilian police force. Three thousand FAd'H were integrated into the Interim Public Security Force (IPSF). Yet it was clear from the outset that the IPSF was 'tainted' and unacceptable as a national police force in the long run. As the HNP grew and cadets graduated, the IPSF was gradually demobilised.[42] Military influence should also be kept out of police training. Military training of police undermines attempts to implement the separation of military and police; this is especially so where there is a legacy of a blurred distinction between the police and the military, for instance in El Salvador or Haiti.

In Kosovo – as in Haiti – financing the police forces remained a problem, as indigenous civil authorities were still in the process of being established and there was little income from taxation to pay for the KPS. In all cases, the local authorities were in dire straits financially and faced tough choices in the wake of the conflicts. For example, 'in order to keep within the IMF spending limits, El Salvador was unable to afford to build a national civil police force *and* to embark on an arms-for-land programme to reintegrate guerrillas as required by the peace agreement'.[43] A balance has to be struck: ultimately, these priorities have to be set by the local authorities. At the same time, however, international actors have to safeguard the values they are promoting and ensure that reform is not jeopardised, for example by local authorities channelling funds to military budgets or private coffers. Needless to say, the insecure fiscal base of the economy and low salaries can increase the temptations of corruption and black market activity and undermine efforts to build a democratic, credible and effective police force.

Structural reform is difficult because it entails (re)-distributing the responsibility for security and is therefore a highly sensitive issue. Former opponents are likely to be distrustful of each other but may be forced to share power, territory and the responsibility for internal security. This was the case in all Balkan theatres, as well as in El Salvador and Mozambique. One particular example is Eastern Slavonia, where the Croatian and Serb population had to learn both to share responsibility for security in a hotly contested area and to trust that security would be non-partisan.[44] In Bosnia-Herzegovina, redistributing security meant reorganising police forces in accordance with the government structures established in the Dayton Agreement. In other words, two police organisations would be formed, one for the Federation and one for the Republika Srpska.

Virtually all cases of police reform – Mozambique, El Salvador, Cambodia, Angola, Kosovo, Eastern Slavonia – have involved bringing about a multi-ethnic or multi-party composition in the police force in order to instil greater confidence among the population and to reflect the ethnic composition of the state. The composition of the police force is important because it has a major impact on the credibility of the force and ultimately on the sustainability of the system.[45] In practice, establishing multi-ethnicity proved difficult and informal structures often dominated the police organisations, so that in Bosnia-Herzegovina, for instance, there were not two forces but in effect three – one for each ethnic group.[46] Another example is the Kosovo Police Service School (KPSS), which placed great emphasis on multi-ethnicity and boasted a satisfactory number of minority recruits (17%, of which 9% were Serb), as well as female recruits (20%).[47] Yet only the ability to retain the desired share of Serb officers in the long term will provide the KPS with the needed legitimacy. Similarly, the International Crisis Group initially saw no evidence of political influence over the recruitment and selection of candidates for the KPSS, but suggested there was a danger of this happening once control over selection has been handed over to local authorities.[48] In contrast, due to an approach that emphasised professionalisation, the police force in El Salvador adopted its new identity easily with little tension between former opponents.[49]

Civpol's role in police reform may be multifarious, ranging from demobilisation to training and selection to advice on organisational and budgetary matters, but it has a clear underlying purpose. In times when there is little trust between former warring parties and there is little faith in the indigenous police forces on the part of the population, international police monitors and trainers provide a critical security guarantee, especially when backed up by an international military force. They also legitimise local public security forces that are generally struggling to prove themselves. This is where the behavioural counterpart to structural reform comes in.

Training and Monitoring the Conduct of Local Police Forces

The second 'prong' in the creation of a democratic police force – instituting behavioural reform – requires processes that are much more difficult to define and assess. In order to promote behavioural reform, UN and other civilian police forces monitor police performance, conduct police training, set up police academies, including curriculum development and the establishment of procedures for recruitment and selection. In addition, the six years of police reform efforts in Bosnia-Herzegovina have led to a more sophisticated approach to training, where international assistance goes to training specialised police forces, such as for border services, crowd control, and criminal intelligence. Similar courses were also held in Haiti after basic training had been completed. These examples of specific skills and the local police's ability to fulfil a wide spectrum of policing tasks also have a structural dimension, in that separate branches are established, for example, in intelligence or border control. Behavioural reform, in contrast, emphasises a change in the way policemen act and in the attitudes that underlie police work, such as how they view the relations between the police and the population, when and how force may be applied, etc.

Perhaps in keeping with the ill-defined nature of behavioural reform, the common denominator of efforts at reforming and restructuring indigenous police forces so far has been the absence of a declared aim. UNTAES exemplifies the problems of an inconsistent approach. As there were very few resources available for training, staff wrote their own teaching materials based on their home country background, which resulted in contradictory instructions, until ICITAP finally stepped in with a curriculum blue print. After that, the benefits of experience and cohesion and unity of approach soon became clear.[50]

Too often, the time it takes to reform, train and deploy an indigenous police force is underestimated. This is especially true for the behavioural aspects of reform, as changing attitudes are far more challenging and time-consuming than restructuring a force. Just as a marker, it is helpful to note that in Kosovo the goal was to train 4,000 officers – later adjusted to 6,000 – and in Haiti approximately 5,000. A rough estimate suggests that it takes at least a year before the first group of officers are ready for a full range of policing activities, including selection/recruitment and academy and field training.[51] Shortcuts, such as those taken in Haiti, have proved counterproductive, where training courses were criticised for being too short to have a lasting effect. This is especially true when there are no role models, local older police officers with significant experience for instance, to guide the behaviour of a fledgling police force. In other words, it takes time – and certainly more than the initial training year – to develop leadership capacity.[52] The importance of mentors was illustrated in Haiti: when the programme that matched international field training officers with young, newly educated Haitian officers ceased with the transition to UNSMIH, the mission lost an effective instrument for consolidating reform. In the same way, the short-lived – and perhaps short-sighted – assistance to the Somali police was doomed to fail, as the foundation created by the handful of police advisors serving with UNITAF was abandoned in UNOSOM II despite the fact that the UN mission had an explicit mandate to 're-establish' the Somali police.[53]

Of all the tasks in behavioural reform, monitoring tends to continue for the longest period of time, as – in most operations – it carries on after the initial restructuring and training has been completed. Non-executive functions do not cease simply because the civilian police takes on an executive role. In Kosovo and East Timor executive policing is concurrent with efforts to establish a functioning indigenous police force, i.e. monitoring and training. It is likely that these executive missions will transform into more limited monitoring missions sooner or later. When UNTAES was wound down after two years and political authority was returned to the Croatian government, the more extensive training role of the civilian police component also ceased. The civilian police component was replaced by the United Nations Police Support Group (UNPSG), which had a pure monitoring mandate. Nine months later, in October 1998, the mandate was passed on to a monitoring group under the OSCE.

Respect for human rights has remained the central monitoring concern in all civilian police operations, whether in Central America, Africa or Europe. Instilling respect for and ensuring the protection of human rights by the local police forces is a crucial task for civilian police and human rights NGOs, as the population's confidence in its security depends to a large extent on its day-to-day contact with the police. Marotta argues that human rights are more acceptable when declared part of a process of professionalisation than when they are seen as a challenge to police work. In other words, training should emphasise that human rights are not simply a legal obligation but part and parcel of being a professional police force and a fundamental element in law enforcement.[54]

The fact that police reform touches on highly sensitive issues and is to some extent a diplomatic activity place high demands on the quality of staff and its ability to develop close ties with the local community. Many cases have shown that the most effective way for civilian police to approach and work with local police is on a collegial and professional basis. In Haiti, the police monitors were co-located with local police as well as with United States Military Police. Similarly, the IPTF in Bosnia-Herzegovina initially lacked clout in its recommendations and reprimands to their counterparts in the indigenous police forces. Closer contact developed and monitoring became more effective, however, when IPTF officers were co-located with their Bosnian colleagues and when SFOR and IPTF conducted joint patrols.[55]

When devising grand plans for how external actors can mould an indigenous police force, one has to remember that a police force is a professional organisation like any other, with a defined occupational culture. This is especially true in the case of Bosnia-Herzegovina, where an existing police force was to be reformed and where the organisational culture of the force was a product of pre-war police experience, as well as the experience of the recent conflict.[56] This is also true of El Salvador, where police represented impunity rather than justice. A discussion on entry points for reform has started and it has been suggested that training the 'right' people in the local hierarchy, such as mid-level management and other power holders, is instrumental to reforming organisational culture successfully. Ideally, this approach should be reflected in the initial design of a mission, in which the main recipients, the focus of training and the most effective strategy for training are identified.[57] Ownership of the reform process is enhanced by developing codes of conduct and operational guidelines in cooperation with indigenous police and by training mid- and senior-level officers. This also follows the reasoning that police reform and human rights training are not simply a matter of teaching a few courses but of changing an institution and its organisational culture.[58]

The experience gained in Albania illustrates the challenge of translating training into effective practical policing, particularly in the light of an unstable political context and widespread crime. The WEU Multinational Advisory Police Element (MAPE) in Albania claimed relative success in creating a professional police force. Challenges, here as elsewhere in the Balkans, arose when the police were released onto the streets and problems of corruption, the spread of illegal weapons and organised crime surfaced.[59] In general, though, structural and behavioural reform processes have been relatively successful. The major difficulty encountered in all cases is the political influence on the police forces. Despite their multi-ethnic composition, ethnic tensions still existed within most forces and were even fostered by the political leadership. Clearly, reform projects are comprehensive and ambitious undertakings and it takes a long time for the revamped police to come into their own. The reformed or newly established police force has to develop its own culture and internal dynamic and control mechanisms. Each society will eventually arrive at a level of order that it considers tolerable in the long run.

Conclusion

Beyond Kosovo

Having taken a closer look at the trials and tribulations of civilian police in peace operations, some critical questions remain. International organisations, first and foremost the UN as the most prolific dispatcher of police to war-torn societies, have embarked on a challenging path. Too often, developments towards highly intrusive operations and the steadily increasing scope of police operations are accepted uncritically. Criticism is directed at the inability to fulfil those missions efficiently rather than at why they are in a given crisis area and whether they should be there at all. But these questions are equally valid: would we have been better off not deploying civilian police? Or worse still: are civilian police operations a waste of time, energy and money? This paper has shown that there have been successes, failures and limited successes. Eastern Slavonia is perhaps the most obvious 'success'. The Namibian 'success story' is typical in that the UN did make a major contribution to establishing a sustainable law and order system but that success remained dependent on 'the full cooperation of the parties, the continuing support of the Security Council, and the timely provision of the necessary financial resources'.[1] In the same way, the results of the operations in Mozambique and El Salvador were consolidated through long-term bilateral police training assistance.

The line between 'successes' and 'limited successes' is not very clear. Initial achievements are in danger of being whittled away in many cases, as we have seen in El Salvador, Haiti and

Bosnia-Herzegovina, due to an adverse political context, widespread corruption and continued poverty and instability. Finally, of the failures, Somalia enjoyed only a brief moment in the sun before joining the less celebrated of UN operations; and Cambodia was a complete misjudgement of local conditions and the resources needed to address them. A word on Kosovo and East Timor is also in order. They appear to be on the right track, not because of the executive policing role, which the UN's international police had considerable trouble filling, but because the establishment of indigenous police forces has been taken more seriously and training and monitoring were conducted accordingly.[2] Nonetheless, it is important to keep in mind that the scope of the missions in Kosovo and East Timor is likely to remain the exception rather than the rule. Indeed, international organisations might do well to focus on those areas in which they have built up significant know-how and expertise, i.e. training and monitoring. This would be a better investment of personnel and resources than struggling to fulfil ambitious plans to provide a full-blown justice system that includes establishing police, courts and prisons, which in turn is one of several prerequisites for successfully engaging in executive policing. Assuming full responsibility for enforcing the law might just be a bridge too far for international civilian police – UN or otherwise.

Improving the odds for the success of a civilian police operation requires two-fold action. On the one hand, measures can be adopted that will make operations smoother and more cost-efficient. The disastrous consequences of unqualified staff point to one of the most glaring operational shortfalls which has persisted even after more than a decade of extensive civilian police deployment. The issue of developing and recruiting staff with specialised skills rather than amassing a large quantity of civilian police that do not understand their role and are not qualified to fulfil certain tasks within the mission has also been discussed above. Choosing a more sophisticated approach to the necessary skills simply means professionalising civilian police for international missions. This is only possible when a clearer understanding of the objectives of different missions and their political implications, as well as the skills required to fulfil them, is also reached. Indeed, even making an assessment as to whether or not a case can be considered a success implies that the contributors and the civilian police officers have understood what they are hoping to achieve. This is where operations often lose their way. A more sophisticated approach also reveals an intricate division of labour between the military peacekeepers and the civilian police force. All cases have demonstrated how critical close cooperation is. Moreover, providing a secure environment – in military terms – and enforcing the law – in police terms – are two sides of the same coin and each can only be achieved through an integrated effort. Better cooperation is in turn cultivated through joint planning and pre-deployment fact-finding conducted by the military *and* police. Joint exercises have also been suggested, and have already been held in limited national contexts, for example in Norway. Both the Brahimi Report and plans for the EU's Crisis Management Mechanism emphasise joint planning and joint exercises.

Another aspect addressed in this paper was the need to develop a better approach to training. More carefully designed training in turn requires a change in awareness surrounding police operations. This is perhaps the greatest obstacle for meeting operational challenges. Only when domestic authorities – including interior, justice, defence and foreign ministries – and development agencies and other domestic police authorities regard the international deployment of police officers as an essential and valuable part of police work will steps be taken to facilitate the recruitment, preparation and, not least, the reintegration of returning policemen. Ideally, this will then lead to a more highly developed and cohesive approach within and between contributing governments. Sadly, the opposite trend is in evidence in the United States, where the recruitment of police for international missions has been passed on to a private corporation, resulting in a lack of quality control and accountability.

The measures suggested so far are operational improvements and serve to enhance police capabilities and promote human rights in daily police practice – an important feat by any standards. Although practical issues may appear staid in the face of wider political questions, they are valuable contributions to enhancing the effectiveness of civilian police operations. It has even been argued that the crux of the Brahimi Report, its practical recommendations and its implications, is a forewarning that unless the UN's capacity to conduct peacekeeping operations and deploy international civilian police is enhanced significantly, there is a danger that the UN will slide into irrelevancy.

The other action to increase the effectiveness of deployments touches on the political context of an operation, the effects of which must clearly be better understood. All cases underlined how progress can be either galvanised or eradicated by the political framework. The Somali case stands out as a prime example of how political opposition can tear up a promising foundation for the rule of law, but numerous other examples could be offered. So the question is whether there are measures that can be taken to render the political context more favourable or to foster consent and support from the local political leadership. This also includes finding a way in which either to gain at least the tacit support of powerful players in informal networks or to combat them and remove their influence. In particular, dealing with so-called spoilers means tackling criminal networks and fighting corruption and the criminalisation of the state.

It is fairly obvious that a more comprehensive system of sanctions and incentives would help these efforts. The clout that international actors can bring to bear on recalcitrant parties is contingent upon the parties' dependence on international assistance. For instance, the international community had more attractive incentives to offer in Bosnia-Herzegovina than they did in Angola.[3] But attempts to take action have most often been foiled by inconsistent political backing among contributors which have made threats appear less threatening and rewards appear less rewarding.

Fostering cooperation with local actors – ranging from the population to the police, informal networks and political authorities – is no easy task and is in no way exclusive to the civilian police. On the contrary, it is so difficult to address that it requires a broad coalition among different actors involved in the peace operation and, more importantly, a cohesive approach to police reform and other reconstruction efforts. The civilian police need the political backing that only agreement among the big players in that coalition, i.e. the United States and Europe, can provide. This in turn requires that civilian police are recognised as an integral and powerful part of the international effort. The improved cooperation between UNMIK, on the one hand, and NATO, the OSCE and the EU, on the other, in Kosovo indicates some progress towards acknowledging the need for an integrated effort. However, power politics between the United States, Europe and to a lesser extent Russia and China, which are played out in all of those organisations, undermine operational cohesion on the ground and underline that cohesion has to be more thorough. An aspect that has not been explored in detail in this paper is the role of regional organisations and bilateral assistance in civilian police operations and police reform. Similar to the predominantly UN operations examined here, there is both potential and danger: while all contributions should generally be welcomed, incorporating a wide range of organisations and individual governments also exacerbates existing problems of coordination and cohesion.

Failure is often easier to identify than success. A recurring and exceedingly difficult question is how we know whether we *have* been successful and if so, *to what extent*. General criteria for measuring success have been and will remain elusive. Goals have tended to be exaggerated, and there is a good argument for being modest. After all, we are not looking to transform war-torn societies into crime-free ones, but to identify and arrive at tolerable levels of crime and instability. Derek Chappell, police spokesman for UNMIK, commented in December 2000 that 'the real fight against fear, violence and intimidation must be fought in the hearts and minds of the people of Kosovo, who must confront this casual acceptance of violence'.[4] While that is true, the tolerance that the population in the Balkans displays for everyday violence might well be unacceptable to an outside observer, but is ultimately subject to an internal assessment within each society. The real goal is to create relatively stable societies in which respect for human rights is self-sustaining.

Civilian police operations are certainly a vital element in a sweeping state-building and transformation exercise. The UN's International Security Assistance Force (ISAF), authorised in December 2001 to assist the Afghan authorities in maintaining security, has a predominantly military focus. But the need to promote the rule of law, i.e. to establish a democratic police force and its corollaries – an independent judiciary and penal institutions and, with time, an active civil society – as the backbone of the regeneration of Afghanistan is obvious and underlines just how essential and how complex civilian police assistance to war-torn societies is. Civilian police operations are a challenge because they are tools both of immediate crisis management and of development assistance and democratisation. As reform projects steadily grow in size and scope, a more poignant question is how to prioritise different aspects on the reform agenda. The key is to reach for an outcome that lies between the likely and the desirable. After all, the attention span of the international community and the funds that it provides are limited. And in the end, there is a need to create something that is tolerable to the locals, sustainable by the locals, and is based on an enduring respect for human rights.

Notes

Acknowledgements

I would like to acknowledge the
support of the Centre for the
Democratic Control of the Armed
Forces, which allowed me to spend
a year at the Institute, working on
this paper. In researching and
writing this paper I have benefited
greatly from numerous
conversations with researchers and
practitioners working on issues
relating to civilian police in peace
operations. While all have
contributed valuable input, I would
like to highlight the conversations
with a number of international
policemen that liberally shared their
experiences from various missions
with me. Finally, I am grateful to
Renata Dwan, Robert Perito and Eric
Scheye for their extremely helpful
and perceptive comments on a draft
of this paper and to my colleagues
at IISS: Mats Berdal, Jane Chanaa,
Paul Lalor and John Peterson.

Chapter 1

1 See for example Rama Mani, 'The
   Rule of Law or the Rule of
   Might? Restoring Legal Justice in
   the Aftermath of Conflict', in
   Michael Pugh (ed.), *The
   Regeneration of War-torn Societies*
   (Basingstoke: Macmillan, 2000).

2 William Stanley, 'International
   Tutelage and Domestic Political
   Will: Building a New Civilian
   Police Force in El Salvador', in
   Otwin Marenin (ed.), *Policing
   Change, Changing Police:
   International Perspectives* (New
   York: Garland Publishing, Inc.,
   1996), p. 43.

3 For a concise historical overview,
   see Erwin A. Schmidl, *Police in
   Peace Operations*, Informationen
   zur Sicherheitspolitik No.
   10/September 1998 (Wien:
   Landesverteidigungsakademie).

4 UN website 'Completed
   Peacekeeping Missions', at
   http://www.un.org/Depts/dpko/
   dpko/co_mission/untagFT.htm#
   Functions.

5 UNDPKO/Civilian Police Unit,
   *Briefing on Civilian Police Unit and
   UNCivPol in UN Missions* (New
   York: Civilian Police Unit, DPKO,
   United Nations, 17 September
   1997), p. 20.

6 Robert Perito, 'The Role of
   International Police in Peace
   Operations' (paper presented at
   the *Cornwallis V Conference
   Analysis for Crisis Response and
   Societal Reconstruction*: Lester B.

Pearson Canadian International Peacekeeping Training Center, Nova Scotia, Canada, 17–20 April 2000), p. 4.

7 Quoted in Cheryl M. Lee Kim and Mark Metrikas, 'Holding a Fragile Peace: the Military and Civilian Components of UNTAC', in Michael W. Doyle, Ian Johnstone and Robert C. Orr (eds), *Keeping the Peace. Multidimensional UN Operations in Cambodia and El Salvador* (Cambridge: Cambridge University Press, 1997), p. 108.

8 John McFarlane, *Civilian Police in Peace Operations* (Working Paper No. 64, Australian Defence Studies Centre: Canberra, Australia, April 2001), p. 10.

9 Schmidl, *Police in Peace Operations*, p. 61.

10 Halvor Hartz, 'CIVPOL: The UN Instrument for Police Reform', in Tor Tanke Holm and Espen Barth Eide (eds.), *Peacebuilding and Police Reform* (London: Frank Cass, 2000), p. 39.

11 Stanley, 'International Tutelage and Domestic Political Will', p. 40f.

12 *Report of the Panel on United Nations Peace Operations* ('Brahimi Report' A/55/305-S/2000/809, New York: United Nations, 2000). The panel was chaired by former Algerian foreign minister Lakhdar Brahimi and made recommendations on how to improve the United Nations' capacity for conducting peace operations.

13 UNDPKO/Civilian Police Unit, p. 18.

14 Rachel Neild, 'Policing the police: reform in war-torn societies', *Conflict, Security & Development* vol. 1, no. 1, 2001, p. 7f.

15 *Ibid.*, p. 37.

16 Rama Mani, 'Contextualising Police Reform: Security, the Rule of Law and Post-Conflict Peacebuilding', in Holm and Eide, *Peacebuilding and Police Reform,*

p. 14; Chuck Call and Michael Barnett, 'Looking for a Few Good Cops: Peacekeeping, Peacebuilding and CIVPOL', *Ibid.*, p. 45. Call and Barnett also point out that this pattern is particularly clear in Central American countries that have been subject to US intervention.

17 However, it also included commando and infantry units that became heavily involved in ethnic cleansing during the war.

18 International Crisis Group, *Kosovo Report Card* (ICG Balkans Report No. 100: Pristina, Brussels, 28 August 2000), p. 12; 'Kosovo Protection Corps chief meets NATO Military Council, seeks aid' (Kosovapress news agency web site, Pristina, in Albanian, 20 July 2001). Two points are worth making in relation to the KPC: firstly, despite the official purpose designated by the international community, the KPC is seen by all Kosovo Albanians as their future fledgling armed forces. Secondly, although there is little official money for the KPC, significant funds are supplied by the vast Kosovo Albanian diaspora network that emerged during the Serb repression of the 1990s as the main source of funding for the shadow state.

19 See for example 'Croatian police force to cut 4,000 posts by end of 2001' (HINA news agency, Zagreb, in English 1449gmt, 28 April 2001); 'Police redundancies in eastern Croatia blamed on Serbs taking up posts' (Croatian Radio, Zagreb, in Serbo-Croat 1100gmt, 7 August 2001).

20 Timothy A. Wilkins, 'The El Salvador Peace Accords: Using International and Domestic Law Norms to Build Peace', in Michael W. Doyle, Ian Johnstone and Robert C. Orr (eds.), *Keeping the Peace. Multidimensional UN*

Operations in Cambodia and El Salvador (Cambridge: Cambridge University Press, 1997), pp. 274, 281.

21 John G. Cockell, 'Coordinating Institutional Responses to Security Challenges in Peacebuilding: Kosovo in the Balkans Context' (Paper presented at the IPA-Conference *Managing Security Challenges in Post-Conflict Peacebuilding*, Ottawa, 22–23 June 2001), p. 14.

22 See for example Lee Kim and Metrikas, 'Holding a Fragile Peace', p. 108f.

23 *Ibid.*, p. 120.

24 *Ibid.*, p. 120.

25 Michael Bailey, Robert Maguire and J. O'Neil G. Pouliot (1998) 'Haiti: Military–Police Partnership for Public Security', in Robert B. Oakley, Michael J. Dziedzic and Eliot M. Goldberg (eds.), *Policing the New World Disorder* (Washington DC: National Defence University Press, 1998), p. 224f.

26 Michèle Griffin and Bruce Jones, 'Building Peace through Transitional Authority: New Directions, Major Challenges', *International Peacekeeping* vol. 7, no. 4, Winter 2000, p. 77.

27 Hansjörg Strohmeyer, 'Collapse and Reconstruction of a Judicial System: The United Nations Missions in Kosovo and East Timor', *American Journal of International Law* vol. 95, no. 1, 2001, pp. 49, 51.

28 Tor Tanke Holm, 'CIVPOL Operations in Eastern Slavonia, 1992–98', in Holm and Eide, *Peacebuilding and Police Reform*, p. 146.

29 See for example Francesca Marotta, 'The Blue Flame and the Gold Shield: Methodology, Challenges and Lessons Learned on Human Rights Training for Police', in Holm and Eide, *Peacebuilding and Police Reform*, p. 76.

Chapter 2

1 Holm,'CIVPOL Operations in Eastern Slavonia, 1992–98', p. 153.

2 Lynn Thomas and Steve Spataro (1998) 'Peacekeeping and Policing in Somalia', in Oakley, Dziedzic and Goldberg, *Policing the New World Disorder*, p. 199.

3 Annika S. Hansen, *International Security Assistance to Peace Implementation Processes: The Cases of Bosnia-Herzegovina and Angola* (PhD Dissertation, Oslo, Norway: University of Oslo, 2000), p. 363.

4 See Cockell, 'Coordinating Institutional Responses to Security Challenges in Peacebuilding'.

5 Thomas and Spataro, 'Peacekeeping and Policing in Somalia', pp. 193f, 200f, 204.

6 Conversations with UNMIK staff, Stockholm, June 2001, and CPD/DPKO staff, New York, November 2000.

7 'Verkauft und Verraten', *Der Spiegel*, 27 August 2001, p. 152.

8 Of course, the Security Council routinely managed to ignore African conflicts. Even the operation in Somalia was only initiated after the country had been without a government for over a year. Thomas and Spataro, 'Peacekeeping and Policing in Somalia', p. 178.

9 James L. Woods, 'Mozambique: The CIVPOL Operation', in Oakley, Dziedzic, and Goldberg *Policing the New World Disorder*, p. 144.

10 *Ibid.*, p. 150f.

11 Neild, 'Policing the Police: Reform in War-torn Societies', p. 19.

12 Thomas and Spataro, 'Peacekeeping and Policing in Somalia', p. 175.

13 Bailey, Maguire and Pouliot,

'Haiti: Military–Police Partnership for Public Security', p. 248f.

14 Espen Barth Eide, Annika S. Hansen, Brynjar Lia, *Security Sector Reform as a Development Issue* (Room Doc #7, OECD/Development Assistance Committee, Task Force for International Peace and Development, Paris, 2–3 June 1999), p. 15f. See also Marotta, 'The Blue Flame and the Gold Shield', p. 74.

15 Holm, 'CIVPOL Operations in Eastern Slavonia', p. 152; Hartz 'CIVPOL: The UN Instrument for Police Reform', p. 29f.

16 Hartz, 'CIVPOL: The UN Instrument for Police Reform', p. 32.

17 Marotta, 'The Blue Flame and the Gold Shield', p. 73 (italics given).

18 Hartz, 'CIVPOL: The UN Instrument for Police Reform', p. 31, 40f.

19 *Ibid.*, p. 31.

20 Marotta, 'The Blue Flame and the Gold Shield', p. 69f.

21 *Ibid.*, p. 87.

22 There is a difference between those officers that return into police service in their home countries and those that were already retired prior to their deployment, which is the case for most United States police officers in international missions.

23 Marotta, 'The Blue Flame and the Gold Shield', p. 76.

24 Brahimi Report, para. 181. Note that military staff does not include NATO troops deployed in SFOR and KFOR.

25 The United States is of course the exception as they recruit a large share of retired police officers.

26 The International Crisis Group recounts the evolution of the UNMIK police. Originally, 3,100 were called for, this number was increased to 6,000; a number impossible to meet and later scaled down to approximately 4,700 of which 3,150 had arrived in-theatre by mid-2000. ICG, *Kosovo Report Card*, pp. 43f.

27 Brahimi Report, para. 119.

28 The EU's Civilian Police Initiative aims to established a stand-by capacity of 5,000 police officers that can be deployed to a conflict area within 30 days. The police officers can either be part of an EU mission and be the corollary to the military capability or be made available to the UN, for instance as a rapid deployment contingent for the early stages of a UN operation.

29 'UN Police in Bosnia. Comment by Jacques Paul Klein', *International Herald Tribune*, 8 June 2001 (http://wwww.iht.com/articles/22192.htm).

30 'Misconduct, Corruption by U.S. Police Mar Bosnia Mission', *Washington Post*, 29 May 2001, p. A01 (http://www.sv-vaznesenje.org/forums/news/posts/1093.html).

31 Conversations with CPD/DPKO staff, New York, November 2000 and London, March 2001.

32 See for example ICG, *Kosovo Report Card*, pp. 4, 44.

33 National differences are also experienced in the logistics and equipment of different national contingents. Whereas some arrive fully equipped, others arrive with no more than the shirt on their backs. This, in turn, has consequences in terms of the need for support from other contingents or from the military forces.

34 Hartz, 'CIVPOL: The UN Instrument for Police Reform', p. 32f.

35 Holm, 'CIVPOL Operations in Eastern Slavonia', pp. 151, 153.

36 Bailey, Maguire and Pouliot,

'Haiti: Military–Police Partnership for Public Security', p. 230.

37 Marotta, 'The Blue Flame and the Gold Shield', p. 78.

38 See http://www.civpol.org/unmik/structure.htm

39 *Ibid.*, p. 12; Cockell, 'Coordinating Institutional Responses', p. 9.

40 Marotta, 'The Blue Flame and the Gold Shield', p. 77f. Marotta cites that the programmes in UNTAES and for the IPTF were the most comprehensive and managed to reach 40% and 36% of international police staff, respectively.

41 When it finally was held, it was with the involvement of the UN Centre for Human Rights and Amnesty International. Woods, 'Mozambique: The CIVPOL Operation', p. 158, 162f.

42 See http://www.civpol.org/unmik/training.htm

43 Lee Kim and Metrikas, 'Holding a Fragile Peace', p. 113ff. Full deployment was reached in November 1992. Lee Kim and Metrikas point out that it took three months to reach 50% and eight months to reach 95% of intended deployment.

44 *Ibid.*, p. 112.

45 Conversation with UNHCR staff, Geneva, April 2001.

46 Alice Hills, 'The Inherent Limits of Military Forces in Policing Peace Operations', *International Peacekeeping* vol. 8, no. 3, Autumn 2001, pp. 86–91.

47 They are not cheaper per person, but governments can for instance get away with seconding a handful of policemen, where an equivalent military contribution might be a few hundred soldiers.

48 On Haiti, see Bailey, Maguire and Pouliot, 'Haiti: Military–Police Partnership for Public Security', p. 251; on Somalia, see Thomas and Spataro, 'Peacekeeping and Policing in Somalia', pp. 187, 205, 212.

49 Hills, 'The Inherent Limits of Military Forces in Policing Peace Operations'.

50 Haiti is one example of earlier peacekeeping operations in which military and police cooperated closely and effectively. Joint patrols in Haiti were nicknamed 'Four Men in a Jeep' and included an international and an indigenous policeman, a military peacekeeper and an interpreter.

51 Thomas and Spataro, 'Peacekeeping and Policing in Somalia', pp. 210, 212. Bailey, Maguire and Pouliot, 'Haiti: Military–Police Partnership for Public Security', p. 250f.

52 Hills, 'The Inherent Limits of Military Forces in Policing Peace Operations', pp. 80ff, 93.

53 Woods, 'Mozambique: The CIVPOL Operation', p. 161.

54 Lee Kim and Metrikas, 'Holding a Fragile Peace', p. 122. In Haiti, the military also assisted in monitoring the HNP. Bailey, Maguire and Pouliot, 'Haiti: Military–Police Partnership for Public Security', p. 234.

55 In early 2001, the UNMIK police were in charge of public safety in three out of the five districts in Kosovo and were responsible for criminal investigations in all five districts. The so-called 'traffic light system', which monitored and recorded violent incidents throughout the area of operation and provided an indicator of the level of tension, was similar to that used in NATO-HQ in Bosnia-Herzegovina. In Kosovo, the UNMIK police retained authority at 'green' and 'orange' levels, but KFOR stepped in when tension climbed to a 'red' level. Conversations with UNMIK

Police staff, Stockholm, May 2001, and Berlin, June 2001.

[56] Hills, 'The Inherent Limits of Military Forces in Policing Peace Operations', pp. 81, 94.

[57] 200 US and 120 Indian military police stayed on under US command during the subsequent UNMIH. Bailey, Maguire and Pouliot, 'Haiti: Military–Police Partnership for Public Security', pp. 227f, 233.

[58] The MSU in Bosnia-Herzegovina consisted of 350 Italian Carabinieri, and minor contributions of Argentinian Gendarmeria Nacional, Romanian Politia Militari and Slovenian Military Police.

[59] Interview with one of the MSU commanders (http://www.nato.int/sfor/indexinf/92/msufor/t0007191.htm).

[60] The primary tasks of the MSU are law enforcement, in particular criminal intelligence on organised crime, and civil disturbances. The Special Police Unit in Kosovo was intended to contribute to the protection of UN staff, to provide operational support and back-up to civilian police, to deal with threats to public order in co-ordination with KFOR and to assist the nascent KPS with crowd control. *Guidelines for Governments Contributing Special Police Units to UNMIK* (New York: CPD/DPKO, 1999), p. 9.

[61] Hills, 'The Inherent Limits of Military Forces in Policing Peace Operations', p. 92f.

[62] Conversations with various UNMIK and UNMIBH staff, London, March 2001, Paris, March 2001, Stockholm, May 2001, Ottawa, June 2001, Berlin, June 2001, and meetings at CPD/DPKO, New York, November 2000.

[63] Conversations with UNMIK staff, Berlin, June 2001. See also

Cockell, 'Coordinating Institutional Responses', p. 22.

[64] For Somalia, see Thomas and Spataro, 'Peacekeeping and Policing in Somalia', p. 210; for Haiti see Bailey, Maguire and Pouliot, 'Haiti: Military–Police Partnership for Public Security', p. 244.

[65] 'Verkauft und Verraten', *Der Spiegel*, 27 August 2001, p. 152.

[66] 'The Role of Police-Military Units in Peace-keeping', (Jane's at http://www.janes.com/police/editors/peacekeeping.htm).

[67] David Holiday, 'Guatemala's Long Road to Peace', *Current History*, February 1997, p. 74.

[68] Thomas and Spataro, 'Peacekeeping and Policing in Somalia', p. 180f.

[69] WOLA, *Demilitarizing Public Order. The International Community, Police Reform and Human Rights in Central America and Haiti* (Washington DC: WOLA, 1995), p. 2.

[70] Marotta, 'The Blue Flame and the Gold Shield', p. 73f; Hartz, 'CIVPOL: The UN Instrument for Police Reform', p. 31.

[71] Marotta, 'The Blue Flame and the Gold Shield', p. 70.

[72] *Ibid.*, p. 81.

[73] Bailey, Maguire and Pouliot, 'Haiti: Military–Police Partnership for Public Security', p. 232.

[74] David A. Lake and Donald Rothchild, 'Containing Fear. The Origins and Management of Ethnic Conflict', *International Security*, vol. 21, no. 2, 1996, p. 42.

[75] Neild writes that technical skills are barely used in Haiti, as they appear to have no relevance to the course of justice. Neild, 'Policing the Police: Reform in War-torn Societies', p. 12.

[76] ICG, *Rule over Law: Obstacles to the Development of an Independent Judiciary in Bosnia-Herzegovina* (ICG, 5 July 1999), p. II. 6f.

Chapter 3

1. Hartz, 'CIVPOL: The UN Instrument for Police Reform', p. 28f.

2. Thomas and Spataro, 'Peacekeeping and Policing in Somalia', p. 179.

3. Brahimi Report, para. 79–83.

4. Neild, 'Policing the Police: Reform in War-torn Societies', pp. 9, 15. For more on democratic control, see Neild, 'Policing the Police: Reform in War-torn Societies', pp. 14–18.

5. Bailey, Maguire and Pouliot, 'Haiti: Military–Police Partnership for Public Security', p. 236.

6. Susan L. Woodward, *Milosevic Who? Origins of the New Balkans* (Discussion Paper No. 5, The Hellenic Observatory, London School of Economics and Political Science: London, 2001), p. 13ff; ICG *Kosovo Report Card*, p. 24.

7. Thomas and Spataro, 'Peacekeeping and Policing in Somalia', pp. 208, 190f, 212f.

8. Hartz, 'CIVPOL: The UN Instrument for Police Reform', p. 37.

9. Neild, 'Policing the Police: Reform in War-torn Societies', pp. 8, 13f. The deployment of International Police Monitors (IPMs) in Haiti was an exception, as police were deployed as national contingents in units or with functional areas of responsibility. Bailey, Maguire and Pouliot, 'Haiti: Military–Police Partnership for Public Security', p. 223.

10. Bailey, Maguire and Pouliot, 'Haiti: Military–Police Partnership for Public Security', p. 227f; WOLA, *Demilitarizing Public Order*, p. 27.

11. Thomas and Spataro, 'Peacekeeping and Policing in Somalia', pp. 182, 206.

12. Woods cites Mozambique as an example of these issues. Woods, 'Mozambique: The CIVPOL Operation', p. 157.

13. Schmidl, *Police in Peace Operations*, p. 12.

14. Perito, 'The Role of International Police in Peace Operations', p. 13. 100,000 Serbs lived in the Sarajevo suburbs and the Civpol Commissioner arrived in late January 1996.

15. Woods, 'Mozambique: The CIVPOL Operation', p. 160.

16. Lee Kim and Metrikas, 'Holding a Fragile Peace', p. 121.

17. ICG, *Kosovo Report Card*, p. 4.

18. Neild cites that 25% of crimes were being reported in 1996. Neild, 'Policing the Police: Reform in War-torn Societies', p. 12f. See also WOLA, *Demilitarizing Public Order*, p. 34; Bailey, Maguire and Pouliot, 'Haiti: Military–Police Partnership for Public Security', p. 217.

19. See for example Neild, 'Policing the Police: Reform in War-torn Societies', p. 2.

20. See Woods, 'Mozambique: The CIVPOL Operation', p. 145

21. Schmidl, *Police in Peace Operations*, p. 11.

22. For example, there are clear and destabilising patterns of crime in Kosovo, but crime rates are by no means excessive. The murder rate in Kosovo was expected to decrease from 13 to 8 per 100,000 in 2001. In comparison, Norway has a significantly lower murder rate at about 0.7 per 100,000, but the rate in the United States as a whole is 5–6 per 100,000 on average, indicating that many cities, such as Los Angeles have a higher rate than that of Kosovo. The murder rate in Russia offers another comparison, with approximately 14 murders per 100,000. Conversation with KFOR staff, London, August 2001.

23. Woods, 'Mozambique: The CIVPOL Operation', p. 145f.

24. Neild, 'Policing the Police: Reform in War-torn Societies', p. 10;

WOLA, *Demilitarizing Public Order*, p. 1f.

25 Mani, 'Contextualising Police Reform', p. 13.

26 Bailey, Maguire and Pouliot, 'Haiti: Military–Police Partnership for Public Security', pp. 245–7.

27 Cited by ICG, *Kosovo Report Card*, p. 2.

28 While the term 'terrorism' should be used with care in the aftermath of the attacks of September 11, 2001, it is still appropriate in the current context in that the core of any definition of 'terrorism' is politically motivated, systematic violence.

29 Graham Day, 'The Training Dimension of the UN Mission in Bosnia and Herzegovina (UNMIBH)', *International Peacekeeping* vol. 7, no. 2, 2000, pp. 158f.

30 Bailey, Maguire and Pouliot, 'Haiti: Military–Police Partnership for Public Security', p. 246.

31 Human Rights Watch, *World Report 2001: Federal Republic of Yugoslavia* (http://www.hrw.org/wr2k1/europe/yugoslavia-kosovo.html); ICG, *Kosovo Report Card*, p. 2, 3.

32 See for example OHR, *Report by the High Representative for Implementation of the Peace Agreement to The Secretary-General of the United Nations* (Sarajevo, Bosnia-Herzegovina: Office of the High Representative, 3 May 2000), para. 43 ff; United States General Accounting Office (GAO), *BOSNIA Crime and Corruption Threaten Successful Implementation of the Dayton Agreement* (Testimony Before The Committee on International Relations, House of Representatives, GAO/T-NSIAD-00–219: Washington DC, 19 July 2000), p. 4; LTC Mac Warner et al., *SFOR Lessons Learned in Creating a Secure Environment with Respect for*

the *Rule of Law* (Carlisle, Pennsylvania: US Army Peacekeeping Institute, May 2000), p. ix.

33 Michael Wesley, 'The Cambodian Waltz: the Khmer Rouge and United Nations Intervention', *Terrorism and Political Violence*, vol. 7, no. 4, 1995, p. 76.

34 Cockell, 'Coordinating Institutional Responses', p. 18. ICG, *Kosovo Report Card*, p. 3. The contenders for a role of the prime security provider can include insurgent militias, state-sanctioned vigilante groups, local paramilitary self-defence leagues, special counter-insurgency forces, secret police units, warlords, and non-political criminal gangs.

35 Lee Kim and Metrikas, 'Holding a Fragile Peace', p. 118.

36 Call and Barnett, 'Looking for a Few Good Cops', p. 44.

37 David Bayley, 'The Contemporary Practices of Policing: A Comparative View', in *Multinational Peacekeeping — A Workshop Series. A Role for Democratic Policing* (National Institute of Justice: Washington DC, October 6, 1997), pp. 3f, 5; Neild, 'Policing the Police: Reform in War-torn Societies', p. 3.

38 See also Otwin Marenin, 'Approaches to Police Reform' (Paper presented at the IISS/DCAF Workshop on Managing the Context of Police Reform, Geneva, 24–25 April 2001).

39 With the exception of ICITAP's efforts, very few operations have included attempts to build administrative and managerial capacity. The ability to manage a police organisation is however critical to long-term self-sufficiency.

40 For a detailed description of police reform efforts in Bosnia-Herzegovina, see Hansen,

International Security Assistance,
pp. 139–149.

41 Efforts were made to gradually
reduce the share of former KLA
— at 40% as of April 2001 — in
the fledgling KPS. Steve Bennett,
'Briefing on the Kosovo Police
School' Presentation at the
IISS/DCAF Workshop on
*Managing the Context of Police
Reform — Implications for
International Assistance*, Geneva,
24–25 April 2001). For more on
the disarmament of the KLA, see
for example, ICG, *Kosovo Report
Card*, pp. 10–14.

42 Bailey, Maguire and Pouliot,
'Haiti: Military–Police Partnership
for Public Security', p. 225f. The
HNP fully replaced the IPSF in
March 1995.

43 Emphasis added. Mary Kaldor,
*New & Old Wars. Organized
Violence in a Global Era* (Stanford,
Cal.: Stanford University Press,
1999), p. 131.

44 A new Transitional Police Force
(TPF) was established for the
region with equal participation of
Serbs and Croats to alleviate fears
of harassment. For the first two
years, from January 1996–98, it
was under the authority of the
UN mission, UNTAES, and
was then integrated into the
structure of the Croatian police
force.

45 Neild, 'Policing the Police: Reform
in War-torn Societies', p. 5.

46 Day, 'The Training Dimension',
p. 158f; GAO, *BOSNIA Crime and
Corruption*, p. 3f.

47 Bennett, 'Briefing on the Kosovo
Police School'.

48 ICG, *Kosovo Report Card*. The
organisational division of labour
is as follows: academy training
of KPS candidates is conducted
by the OSCE; field training and
continuous supervision is in
the hands of the UNMIK
police.

49 Neild, 'Policing the Police: Reform
in War-torn Societies', p. 5.

50 Holm, 'CIVPOL Operations',
p. 147.

51 Hartz, 'CIVPOL: The UN
Instrument for Police Reform',
p. 33.

52 Mani, 'The Rule of Law', p. 14;
Bailey, Maguire and Pouliot,
'Haiti: Military–Police Partnership
for Public Security', pp. 235, 243.

53 Thomas and Spataro,
'Peacekeeping and Policing in
Somalia', pp. 205–7.

54 Marotta, 'The Blue Flame and the
Gold Shield', pp. 72, 86, 88.

55 Hansen, *International Security
Assistance*, p. 141.

56 ICG, *The Policing Gap: Law and
Order in the New Kosovo
(International Crisis Group, 6
August 1999)*, p. 8. This raises the
question of whether it is easier to
reform an existing police force or
to 'start from scratch'. Case study
evidence shows that there can be
no simple answer: Whereas
Kosovo is a strong argument in
favour of starting afresh, the
Haitian case illustrates all the
difficulties of building a police
force in the absence of policing
traditions, established doctrine
and culture and experienced
senior officers. Clearly, progress
depends more on the political and
socio-economic context of reform
than on the prior existence of an
indigenous police force.

57 Marotta, 'The Blue Flame and the
Gold Shield', p. 75.

58 Marotta, 'The Blue Flame and the
Gold Shield', pp. 80–3; Marenin,
'Approaches to Police Reform'.

59 Conversations with MAPE
officers, Paris, March 2001, and
Stockholm, May 2001. Also
'Council of Europe praises
positive progress of police reform
in Albania' (ATA news agency,
Tirana, in English, 1600 gmt, 27
July 2001).

118 *Annika S. Hansen*

Conclusion

[1] United Nations Department of Peacekeeping Operations, Completed Missions Information (http://www.un.org/Depts/dpko/dpko/co_mission/untagFT.htm#functions).

[2] Naturally, Kosovo fares better than East Timor in the sense that it is more in the public eye and receives far more funds than East Timor does.

[3] Hansen, *International Security Assistance*, pp. 334, 364.

[4] United Nations Mission in Kosovo, *News Reports* (http://www.un.org/peace/kosovo/news/kosovo2.htm, 11 December 2000).